HOW TO THINK STRAIGHT

by
James D. Weinland

About the Author

1. The author is Professor Emeritus of Business Psychology at New York University. He is now occupied in research and writing.

2. The author has written numerous articles and several books. His principal fields of interest have been thinking, learning, remembering. He has counseled with many students on their methods of study, an inquiry that contains, and has contributed to, the present work.

About the Book

This book developed out of thirty years of teaching the psychology of thinking and ten years of teaching logic. It has had many seasons of growth and pruning. Most of its teenage escapades have been forgotten.

In making its debut now, the book explains in a simple way the development and sharpening of the tools of thought from the days of the early Greeks to the present day. It identifies the major problems all men face and indicates how they can be resolved. It points out many common fallacies of thinking in every day life.

It is offered with the hope that it will complement the information of the reader, increase his insight, and arouse him to learn still more about the tested methods of solving problems.

HOW TO
THINK STRAIGHT

by

JAMES D. WEINLAND

Professor Emeritus
of Business Psychology
New York University

1966

LITTLEFIELD, ADAMS & CO.

Totowa, New Jersey

Printed in the United States of America

Preface

Many, many years ago, people began trying to think straight to useful conclusions. This quest brought insight into the modes of thinking. The elements of thought were recognized and their means of organization discovered. Percepts, concepts and generalizations became intelligible tools to explain the relationship of fact to theory. The methods of induction and deduction led to the development of science and the application of knowledge to the needs of men. The fusion and compounding of facts in everyday life led to the necessary use of statistics. The reader will find related these steps of development.

How this background of knowledge can be readily put to use is demonstrated in a discussion of five fundamental problems. Creative thinking is analyzed; its achievement explained. The subordinate nature of one's own experience to the accumulated experience of the human race is shown with instructions so that the reader can find help in resolving his own difficulties. The requirements of making good choices leading to sound decisions are presented. The problems of "how to do it" are made clear with a presentation of the uniform requirements underlying all procedures. Then, after a problem is solved, the process of explaining the conclusion is shown.

Finally an exposition of the most common mistakes in thinking points out to the reader areas of weakness where every thinker should be wary.

This book, as all books do, will have its blemishes. Some of the black spots, however, have been removed with the help of friends. Grateful thanks are rendered to all the many students and associates who have contributed but whom it is impossible to name. Space must be made, though, for a few individuals. Dr. Israel Knox, Associate Professor of Philosophic Studies at New York University, helped clarify some technical problems. Professor Rudolph Lagai advised and encouraged when the work was new. Professor Maurice Trotta and Professor Charles Ray helped with the problem of definition, particularly as related to the law.

Dr. Arbie Dale as well as Dr. Peter Dubno listened to queries on certain problems and helped to solve them. My brother, Clarence, contributed information on creative thinking. Dr. Norton B. Crowell of the University of New Mexico read the entire manuscript with particular reference to the chapter on statistics and suggested changes in English. Dr. Lawrence Brennan introduced the author to the publisher. Mrs. Russell Kink typed the manuscript and helped with its presentation. To all of these, many thanks.

CONTENTS

CONTENTS

Chapter 1

THINKING COMES FROM EXPERIENCE

Thinking is a mental activity of a trial-and-error nature that precedes physical action. It occurs when the next step to be taken is unknown because some difficulty interferes with action. In such cases imaginary trials point the way to a solution, thus preventing unwise responses. An instance is that of Sir James Dewar, the chemist, when he was frustrated by the difficulty of keeping gas cold enough to remain in liquid form. The idea occured to Dewar that if his gases were packaged in a vacuum, which is a general non-conductor, they might remain cold. This device solved his problem and lead, as well, to the familiar thermos bottle.

Thinking is a complex activity. It consists of three elements: percepts, concepts, and generalizations, together with the processes that relate them, induction and deduction. There are also subordinate processes such as classification and the production of hypotheses.

Although thinking is the best way to solve problems it has several competitors for the opportunity to do so. We will examine these substitutes before eliminating them from our discussion.

SUBSTITUTES FOR THINKING

Magic. Magic is a pretense that problems are solved by means of charms. Such superstitions have been universal among ignorant people. Incantations have been called upon to make governments successful, crops grow, trade prosper and illness disappear.

Wherever knowledge has increased, however, the reliance upon magic has decreased. In the most civilized countries magic is no longer called upon to run governments or operate large corporations. Incantations lead one away from the necessary work of observing facts and thus disrupt the process of thinking.

Fatalism; Astrology and Palmistry. By implying that a man's fortunes are predetermined, fatalism discourages thinking. Astrology, a supposed method of determining one's fate by the position of the stars at the time of one's birth was brought to Greece from the East in the fourth century B.C. It has since spread through the West. One's horoscope is based upon a "chart" of the sky at the time of his birth, showing the positions of the stars in relation to the twelve "houses" or formations through which the stars pass. The major star ascendant when one is born is supposed to determine the solution of his problems. Although science has long proven that astrology is without supporting evidence, a great many people still seek the advice of its practitioners. In the United States alone, more than twenty-five hundred astrologers are said to be charging for their services some two hundred million dollars each year. Palmistry is closely related to Astrology. The assumption of the palmist is that one's entire life, including the part not yet lived, can be read in the lines of the hand. Such opinions of a predetermined life imply that thinking might not be as useful as consulting a palmist. Science has proven that this assumption is misleading, but old superstitions are not easily forgotten.

Dreams. Some people believe that the solution of difficulties is to be found in dreams. A familiar example is that of the Egyptian Pharaoh who dreamed of seeing seven fat cows come out of a river followed by seven lean cows. The lean cows ate the fat cows but still remained lean. This achievement was repeated by seven withered ears of corn that consumed seven full ears. Joseph of the Israelites interpreted this dream to mean that seven years of plenty were coming, to be followed by seven years of famine for which the Egyptians had better prepare.

It is said that dreams must be constructed out of the ideas in the mind of the dreamer, consequently it is possible that some dreams form a kind of semi-conscious thinking. But the interpretation of dreams has been a very unreliable guide to the practical affairs of life.

Luck. Dependence upon luck, as in gambling, is a gesture of helplessness. One who makes a decision by tossing a penny, or refuses to travel West on Mondays, or gives up a project because a black cat has crossed his path, or carries a rabbit's foot or a horseshoe for good luck has replaced an opportunity to think with submission to the unknown.

Escape. Escape solves some problems, such as getting out of a burning house, running away from an attack, or leaving a damp climate to improve one's health. But running away does not solve a problem that is within the person himself. Human beings often attempt to escape from reality by daydreaming, ignoring difficulties in this way or finding in the pleasure of fantasy a compensation for the irritations of life. But running away is a temporary expedient which often makes one's troubles worse.

Rationalization. In rationalization we have a mental process that imitates an aspect of true thinking. A person who is rationalizing begins with a conclusion which he tries to justify. The reasoning used here is not objective. The conclusion is something the individual wants to believe. He distorts facts to make the desired conclusion appear to be sound. For example, President Woodrow Wilson, attending the Versailles conference at the conclusion of World War I, was so anxious to end all wars that he allowed himself to believe that this purpose could be accomplished by the elimination of secret diplomacy and the self-determination of peoples. When the bitter attacks of European statesmen, defending their local interests, led to the rejection of his plans by the United States Senate, President Wilson was brought back to reality, but left a disillusioned man.

Suggestion and Autosuggestion. Suggestion is the art of making action appear easy and attractive in order to get the desired responses without any skeptical thinking by the person involved. Suggestion is used by a doctor when he tells a patient that a few little pills will make him quite well again. The old phrase "putting one's best foot forward" means using suggestion on other people; it is an attempt to camouflage contradictory facts. Whenever, without using authority, a person tries, by concealing all objections, to persuade another person that an action is easy and desirable, he is using suggestion. In presenting only one side of the question he uses suggestion rather than asking for thought.

Autosuggestion is the effort to strengthen oneself by obtaining the cooperation of his unconscious or half-conscious mental processes. It is done by the frequent repetition of certain facts. Andrew Carnegie, as a little boy walking home in the dark, told himself over and over again that, like the legendary Scottish hero, Bruce, he must be brave. Some people whistle in the dark. The formula that the French psychotherapist Emile Coue taught his patients is the most famous example of autosuggestion. They were to repeat twenty times each morning and twenty times each evening, "Day by day in every way I am getting better and better." If they wished a particular ill to disappear their ailment was named in the formula. "Day by day in every way my eyesight is getting better and better." Many people appear to benefit by such techniques, but autosuggestion is rather hoping or believing than thinking.

Positive and Negative Thinking. Positive thinking is an activity that includes a great deal of autosuggestion. It begins with an intent to be biased in a positive manner. One usually recommends positive thinking for people who do not have enough initiative or self-confidence. It is an attempt to change a person rather than to solve a problem. For example, John has always been too cautious, too fearful. He fails because he anticipates failure. John should make an effort to become more optimistic. If he could learn to anticipate success as he now does failure, he would be more successful.

Negative thinking—which is usually referred to as caution— is the type of thinking needed by people who have done too much positive thinking. Young people often fall into this category. Frank sees the world in rosy hues. Everything appears possible. It is taken for granted that he will graduate from college and become successful in his profession. He expects to climb the ladder of success without opposition, forgetting the large number of fellow ladder-climbers. His overconfidence leads him to venture, without adequate preparation, "where angels fear to tread."

Positive and negative thinking are not true thinking although they may be useful when recommended by a psychiatrist, preacher, or friend, for a biased personality. A person should separate autosuggestion from reasoning to understand thoroughly what he is doing. When confronted with a specific problem he should examine all the facts in order to think realistically.

THE ELEMENTS OF THINKING— PERCEPTS, CONCEPTS, GENERALIZATIONS

Percepts. Although percepts are the elementary units of thinking, they are not the most elementary experiences of human beings. A percept is a compound consisting of sensation and memory. When a person hears a voice and recognizes it as his mother's voice, he associates a sense experience with a previous similar experience and thus perceives.

Some of our first learning is of percepts. The child soon says, "Mamma," "Daddy," or "Johnnie." These are all proper names for the child; they are "sign words" for him, pointing to one individual. Such perceptions form the first level of our meaningful thought from which a person begins to make a continuous experience of life. Whenever one recognizes something, he says, in effect, that he has seen it before.

Sensation. The sensations such as sight, sound, smell, and temperature that inform our brain of the world around us, precede memory in experience. These sense reports are interpreted by being associated with other experiences of a similar kind which the individual remembers. As adults we can usually recognize and relate every sensory experience that comes to us. When we do have strange sensations we are puzzled. A noise we do not understand disturbs us until it can be explained. The recognized sensations form the percepts which we use in thinking.

Some people have believed that facts derived from sensation are not reliable. René Descartes, the famous French philosopher of the seventeenth century, gave an oft-quoted example. He heated a cold, hard piece of beeswax which had the odor of honey. Slowly the heat softened the wax to a liquid. Even its odor changed. But all the time it was wax. Obviously, said Descartes, the sense organs cannot be depended upon. At one time they tell us that wax is a hard substance, then a soft substance, and then a liquid. When they change their report on the same substance how can the sense organs be thought to give us reliable information about reality? The modern reader might understand this argument better if he considered walking a mile. In the morning, when walking for exercise, the mile might seem very short. When tired out after a days work the mile would probably seem long. Prisoners walking the "last mile" to the gallows are said to find it no distance at all.

We know today, however, that if conditions are held constant, the sense organs give us reasonably dependable information regarding these constant conditions. Wax of a certain temperature is always hard, at another temperature it is always soft. The bar of metal in the Bureau of Standards in Washington that is a meter long at a given temperature is always exactly one meter long at that temperature. Our sense organs can be relied on if we maintain constant conditions during an observation that is repeated for verification.

Even in illusions our senses make identical reports to identical conditions. People have died in the desert believing they saw a body of water only a short distance away. If one will repeat the observation at the same spot with the sun shining on the sands from the same angle, he will "see" the water, apparently still there. The center lines of the figures below are the same length, although they do not appear so. As long, however, as the figures are drawn in this manner, the illusion of unequal length will remain.

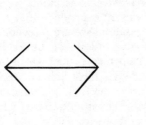

By looking, listening, smelling, or touching repeatedly under the same conditions; by assisting our sense organs with telescopes, microscopes, and other instruments; by using measurements to record our sensations, we determine reality such as it is under certain described conditions. In this way we determine facts that will be true as long as the conditions remain constant.

Memory. In order to think with the facts discovered by our sense organs, we must store them away until we need them. The best way to do this is to record our observations at the time we make them. Unfortunately, we often fail to do this. Near the end of the thirteenth century, Marco Polo spent seventeen years in China, a country that, at that time, was almost unknown to the rest of the world. However, the great Venetian explorer failed to record his observations until years later. Today, no one is sure whether his writing is fact or fiction. A good scientific observer records events when they occur, as did Charles Darwin on his voyage around the world on the Beagle.

Most of us, trusting our memories, never record our experiences at all. But we should at least be aware of the hazards we run. Our memories fail us in at least five ways.

First, there are the inaccuracies due to incomplete observations. Suppose one is questioned about an accident he saw while standing on the street corner when the traffic officer nearby was injured by a hit-and-run driver. He saw it, but he saw only part of it. What was the age of the driver? Memory says, "He looked young, like a teen-ager." What was the color of the car? Memory says, "it was gray." What time was it? "It must have been about five minutes after twelve. I was just going to lunch." However, other witnesses of the same accident may report different facts. Our memories have little reliability when reporting the details of dramatic, rapidly occurring experiences. We often substitute details such as the color of the car or the age of the driver from probabilities, prejudices or the memory of other experiences. Perhaps, also, we forget that we worked late on that particular day before going to lunch.

An illustration of inadequate observation with a consequent poor memory for what happened is found in the experience of Lt. Henry M. Robert of the United States Army Engineers stationed at Bedford, Massachusetts in 1862. It was Robert's duty to act as chairman of a group of citizens engaged in supporting the North in the Civil War. But the meetings went on in such confusion that Lt. Robert could neither accurately observe what was taking place nor recall it correctly. He was so embarrassed in making his reports to Washington that, some years later, he wrote the now famous Robert's Rules of Order. These rules, by improving controlled observation and, consequently, recall of what goes on in a democratic assembly, have become standard. The book still sells more than fifty-thousand copies a year, a hundred years after it was written. We have here adequate proof that thinking is improved when situations are made orderly and recall is improved.

Mental preoccupation can also keep us from observing experiences completely or reporting them correctly. A clinical psychologist about to administer a battery of tests may think of tests when he hears the word "battery," even though the speaker may be referring to the battery in an automobile. Likewise, the word "strike" may have entirely different connotations to a bowler than to a baseball player or a union leader.

Sometimes we are presented with a situation which we do not remember clearly because we fail to understand it. For example, a tourist goes to witness a ceremonial Indian dance. Every motion the dancers make has a meaning to be long remembered by the Indians so that it can be repeated on other occasions, but to the tourist the whole dance seems to consist of senseless confusing noise. The memory of the tourist is so poor that he cannot describe the occasion an hour after he has left it. Or, again, we find the American hero, Hadji Ali, who has been overlooked by most historians because they do not fully understand the service he rendered. Hadji was a Syrian Moslem who left his country to serve the United States Government. He was the caretaker of camels brought, as an experiment, to the Southwest. The camels needed expert care which native born Americans were not qualified to give. In the Beale expedition of 1857, that opened a wagon road across Arizona to California, these camels, under the care of "Hi Jolly," as the American soldiers called him, did excellent service. During the remainder of his life Hadji never saw his native home again. He still continued to work loyally for the United States Government after his beloved camels were released. Today, even though a large monument near Quartzite, Arizona, commemorates his useful work he is so nearly forgotten that his memorial monument is looked upon largely as a curiosity.

A second major difficulty is that we often forget to refer to our memories when necessary. Ideas do not necessarily come to mind spontaneously when we need them most. For instance, Kate Smith, the well-known American singer had to be shocked into recalling the necessity of preserving her health. Kate had starred in over ten thousand radio shows, made over a thousand television appearances, recorded over two thousand songs, earning in her singing career more than thirty-five million dollars. During World War II she travelled nearly fifty-two thousand miles to sing for soldiers and sailors. She sold five hundred million dollars worth of war bonds, she sponsored a Red Cross drive for the donation of blood, and she was continuing the pace.

During the whole period Kate had refused to relax even though she knew her candle was burning at both ends. The idea of danger to her health never came forcefully to mind at the right moment. Then one day Kate's manager had a heart attack. Seeing him lie in an oxygen tent trying to breathe was the effective reminder. The heart attack of Kate's manager signalled her own retirement.

A third difficulty with our memories is that they sometimes refuse to give up what they hold because certain facts have been suppressed. In these cases we banish from our minds embarrassing or shameful experiences that we cannot face. A person who has committed a murder sometimes "blacks out," forgetting the whole incident. A long period of aided recall, as in psychoanalysis, may bring back the memories that are necessary to the solution of a personal problem. Sometimes such memories are never reached.

The fourth reason why our memories fail is associational blocking, as when we cannot think of the name Gordon, because we remember, instead, the name Borden. When we have stage fright, we are so preoccupied with our fear that we forget our speech. We become discouraged because, recalling our failures, we forget our successes. On the other hand, when we feel optimistic we cannot remember any obstacles to our aims; thus people do foolish things when the world looks so bright that their memories fail to bring up the warnings that have been given them.

Another problem is the change in cues by which we bring our memories to mind. We learn the name of a man working in a hardware store only to forget it when he transfers to a candy store. We read facts in a textbook which we fail to recall in solving actual problems.

As a fifth point we have faulty memories because, in living, we are constantly changing them. Every year, for instance, we improve our life histories by adding, or subtracting, a few details. Without conscious intention we minimize our failures and magnify our successes. We should take a cautious or skeptical attitude toward the information given us by our memories.

The Inadequacy of Percepts. The particular triangle you see here is a percept.   Such a percept is a sensory experience related by memory to other experiences. It might appear that perceptions would be adequate to the needs of thought. But since thinking is more than recognition this is not so. A percept brings to mind local associations only since it is tied down to a particular object such as the triangle above. A more striking example of a percept is the experience one has in seeing such a natural wonder as Niagara Falls. Reading about the Falls seems but a shadow compared with being in their presence. Memories of other falls may give contrast to the sights and sounds of Niagara but the actual experience of being there is unique. Sensing Niagara's fury is not thinking. In its elementary form it is merely perception. The essence of thinking is found in relationships; in the abstraction and generalization that often follow a perception. When the person who listens to Niagara tries to calculate the power spent by the falling waters, or when he reflects on the diminutive nature of his own life, he is thinking.

Perceived Objects Change. Another limitation with the use of percepts in thinking is that the objects they represent are always changing. Shoes wear out. Buildings become unrecognizable because they are remodeled. Joe is not the man he was ten years ago. The Greek philosopher Heraclitus (fl.ca. 500 B.C.) was tremendously impressed with the inevitability of change. "A man cannot step into the same river twice," he said. The river would have changed, the man would have changed, indeed everything in the world would have changed between the two steps. Heraclitus believed the problem a man was trying to solve would change into something else before he could reach a conclusion. Thinking exclusively on the level of percepts is impossible. But percepts do form one phase of the thought process by attaching it to an earthly reality, and from percepts concepts are formed.

The Nature of Concepts. One answer to these twin problems of uniqueness and change was offered by Pythagoras (ca. 582-507 B.C.) Pythagoras discovered the universality and permanence of numbers. Any number three, for example, is like any other number three and "lives forever." Even the pyramids, whose present value is that of curious relics, are wearing down. Ancient cities are forgotten. But the number three, universal in its application to any three objects, is perpetually modern. So impressed was Pythagoras with this universal quality and permanence of numbers that his conclusion was "numbers rule the universe."

Obviously numbers, which can be related to any collection of objects, as well as abstract ideas such as "automobile," which can be used to describe many individual cars, are different from percepts which relate to but one object. A class of objects, such as "house," "hat," and "dog," represents an idea that has no physical counterpart. These ideas and classifications are creations of the mind. Since only objects have a physical existence there is, except for the word, no such thing as an objective three. Beauty is not an object. Beauty has no weight nor size; it cannot be packed in a box or carried by the mails or sent by Railway Express. Beauty is not an object, it is an idea. There is no such thing as a generalized automobile. There is only the idea of a group of objects named "automobiles" which has class members that are individual cars. This idea of a class made up of numerous individual instances is called a concept. We have a concept of a man when it is a generalized idea of him conforming to all of his various appearances.

Plato, who followed Pythagoras by about a hundred years, spent much of his time examining language concepts which he found to have the same attributes of universality and permanence as did the number concepts. Such permanent ideas as those representing beauty, freedom, and justice, thought Plato, must be of fundamental importance in the universe. Because Plato did not know where our universal ideas originated or how they are formed, he concluded that we remember them from some former existence. Today they are explained as attributes that have been abstracted from our percepts of a number of similar objects. In the concept of weight we have the attribute of "gravity pull" that can be abstracted from every object in this world. Concepts, such as that of "chair," are more limited and relate to only a few things.

We develop concepts from the objects we meet in our environment by abstracting their various qualities and classifying them. Some of the figures, in the example that follows, will exemplify a particular concept, others will not. Those that meet the requirement of the concept will be marked plus; those that do not will be marked minus. The reader may try, if he wishes, to see how soon he recognizes the characteristics of the concept represented. A definition of the concept, which is given a name, follows the group of figures.

Figures illustrating the concept are marked plus, others are marked minus

The concept represented is that of two straight lines intersecting each other. It will be helpful to name this idea if we hope to use it in conversation or thought. Let us name it an "intersect." All of our concepts were originally formed in much the same way as we have formed the concept of the intersect. People witnessed situations in which fair play was done and others in which it was not done. Finally someone formed the concept of justice, named it, and defined it. But let us return to the intersects.

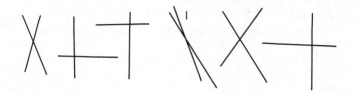

These are all intersects

It will be observed of the intersects that none of them is "the intersect." In the same way, many people are Americans, but none of them is "the American." There are many triangles, but nothing properly called "the triangle." There are many dogs and many cats, but nowhere "the dog" or "the cat." Our intersect is an abstraction, even though it represents some of the qualities of a number of real objects.

The permanence and usefulness of concepts can be well illustrated with triangles. Knowledge about triangles has accumulated since the days of the early Greeks. The concept of the triangle is basic to geometry, since it is the simplest polygon and since, therefore, a theory of measurement for triangles provides a basis for a similar theory for all polygons. The concept of the triangle has led also to trigonometry, which has proved itself invaluable in engineering and other sciences requiring measurement.

High-Level and Low-Level Concepts. Percepts always require the presence of objects. It is impossible to perceive Jack and Jill unless they are present. Concepts, however, do not require the presence of objects. One can think conceptually about Jack or Jill in their absence. Such concepts are made up of the fused memories of many experiences with Jack and Jill. They do not represent the Jack and Jill of one particular observation; the concept is a "composite photograph." Yet, even when we think of these two persons in their absence the concepts of *Jack* and *Jill* refer directly to these two persons. They are called "low-level" concepts, closely resembling percepts, and near the "ground" of actual experience.

Now let us assume that Jack was born in Texas and Jill was born in California. Jack, we say, is a Texan and Jill a Californian. The concepts of *Texan* and *Californian* are more general and less closely related to immediate experience than are the concepts of Jack and Jill. We may therefore say that *Californian* and *Texan* are "higher-level" concepts than *Jack* and *Jill*.

Texans and Californians are citizens of the United States, of whom there are many more than there are Texans or Californians. *Therefore, citizens of the United States* is a higher-level concept than *Texan* or *Californian*. Citizens of the United States can be called North Americans since they live usually on the continent of North America. We have here a concept of still higher-level. North Americans are human beings, just as are people born on other continents. All human beings are *vertebrates*, all vertebrates are *animals*. We have thus arrived at "higher and higher" concepts. Each higher-level concept applies to a larger number of individuals and thus gives wider associational value, but provides less specific information about Jack and Jill.

Our opinion of Jack comes from our experiences with him rather than from reading a book. Low-level concepts based on actual percepts of individual things make up, for the most part, what we call our practical experience. A great deal of "knocking around" in the real world of objects gives a man a good store of low-level concepts. His acts are usually timely because, living in close contact with material things, he modifies his ideas of them as he sees them change. As Jack grows up, the concept that one holds of his personality is frequently remade.

Low-level concepts have obvious referents in the physical world. When we talk of Jack, we do not get him confused with Tom, Dick, or Harry, or Jill. Thus, for each concept of the lowest level there is just one referent. This close association with physical experience brings with it, however, two limitations. One of these is that being at the threshold of sensory experience they suffer from the unreliability of the senses. The second difficulty is that they provide only local associations. We may compare Jack and Jill with Frank and Mary, all of whom we know. When we see Jack and Jill tumbling down the hill, however, we are not likely to be reminded of Dr. Schweitzer and Queen Elizabeth. There is usually nothing in our experience to stimulate such a big associative jump. The imagination of the practical man seldom crosses any extreme gaps since he usually stays reasonably close to the percepts found in his daily work.

As a generalization, it may be said that as concepts get higher they carry more of the distilled experience of the human race since they are less dependent upon the experience of any one person. We need to mention but a few of the highest level concepts—justice, mercy, truth, beauty, power, God— to realize that we did not create these ideas for ourselves out of our own experience but that we got them vicariously from our education. They are the continuous elements of our culture.

High-level concepts last a long time and have wide distribution. Their longevity, however, can cause them to lose touch with reality. Men, for example, are still honoring Pythagoras with their sacred sevens and their dangerous thirteens, even though they know the origin of these concepts. Likewise, a concept can become practically meaningless from disuse. Few people today know exactly what is referred to when one says, "as dead as a dodo." Concepts such as that of freedom have been given, from long and varied use, a whole spectrum of meanings from privileges granted by a king, to moral anarchy.

It is not to be forgotten, however, that, although high-level or universal concepts may be subject to various interpretations, they may also be an advantage in imaginative thinking. Such concepts as freedom enable us to improve social institutions by clarifying political theory.

Many high-level concepts are drawn from other abstractions and consequently have no close physical referents. Thus, the idea of morality is derived from the characteristics of the various virtues, each of which is derived from a more local response. Since the primary function of concepts is to relate experience, however, value is attributed to high-level concepts even when they have no direct objective referents. Thus, the concept of morality leads to the examination of many activities with a consequent integration of information and improvement of judgment.

Summary. The first two elements we use in thinking, then, are percepts and concepts. The lower-level concepts come directly from personal contact with things and help to form our practical experience; the higher-level concepts come largely from our education and carry the culture of the civilized world. Characteristic difficulties come from a lack of either low-level or high-level concepts. The young scholar may have a great supply of high-level concepts, or abstract ideas, which he has obtained from books and lectures, but he may be poorly supplied with low-level concepts from actual experience. He may have good ideas but have difficulty in applying them because of his lack of worldly knowledge. On the other hand, the practical man, with much experience, has a rich store of percepts and low-level concepts, but he has difficulty in relating them and using them creatively. He is not imaginative. He is most successful where the situation calls for standard practice. In a new or complicated situation he is likely to be helpless. When our economy jolted to a stop in the 1930's, Roosevelt called on a "Brain Trust" of imaginative men with high-level concepts to get it started again. Both low- and high-level concepts are needed if problems are to be solved. This is what the philosopher Immanuel Kant had in mind when he said: "Percepts without concepts are blind; concepts without percepts are empty."

Generalization. In considering the elements of thinking we have examined percepts and concepts. We come now to generalizations. Generalizing is a fundamental process of relating ideas by identifying some similarity among them. Generalization is used even in producing percepts when similar sense experiences are associated so that a present instance is recognized as representing a previous occurrence. A perception might be called a low-level generalization as when one says, "John, you are back to your usual self today." Generalizing is used again in forming a concept out of many percepts when they are associated to form a class. Conceiving might then be called "mid-level generalizing." Finally, generalization is used when stating some rule, principle or law descriptive of a uniform element that characterizes a class. It is this last and complex usage—as a synonym for rule or principle—with which most people are familiar.

Generalizations, then, may be on a very elementary or a very advanced level. On the lower level, animals generalize when they are conditioned. In his classical conditioning experiment, the physiologist Pavlov demonstrated that saliva will flow in the mouth of a dog when it sees meat. This is a response to a percept. Then by ringing a bell just before the meat was shown, Pavlov demonstrated that saliva will flow in the mouth of the conditioned dog, before the meat is shown, when the bell rings. Finally, Pavlov demonstrated that it was not necessary always to use the same bell. Any bell reasonably like the original one would do. The dog had generalized a rule of conduct as surely as if he had said, "Whenever I hear the dinner bell, I will salivate for meat."

Generalizations are used both in producing percepts and concepts and in relating them to each other. In relating concepts, particularly at higher levels, it becomes increasingly difficult to make sure that the generalizations used are sound. It is easy to verify simple generalizations such as, "This is a dinner bell." It is more difficult to verify such statements as, "Opportunities do not wait." It is very difficult indeed to test all the elements in such a generalization as Einstein's Theory of Relativity.

When no verification is attempted it is very easy, and usually inaccurate, to generalize. "All Eskimos have good teeth," "A little exercise is always good for you," "The life of a soldier is full of adventure," are probably false statements. Such untested generalizations can be very misleading and bring us to the crux of the problem of thinking.

To think accurately we must determine the facts, that is, make sure that the percepts are free of sensory or memory errors and adequately represent the entire situation. Next, we must be sure that the concepts derived from the percepts are the ones that properly apply. Finally, we must make sure that our generalizations are sound. With this done our tools for thinking are complete.

An interesting example of these elements put together in an effort to solve a problem is the thinking done by the American philosopher John Dewey when he tried to explain the usefulness of the pole with the gilded ball.* Mr. Dewey reported crossing a river every day on his way to work. As he rode the ferry he happened to notice that a long white pole with a gilded ball at its end was projecting from the upper deck. In observing this pole, he formed a percept of it. He noticed its whiteness, its gilt paint and the roundness of the ball at the end. But he did not understand the relationship of the pole or the ball to other things. What were they used for?

He began to associate this particular pole with similar poles he had seen on other boats. The pole thus became a member of a class of such poles.

He made several efforts to identify the class. Could the poles be flagpoles? No, he thought, not flagpoles because such poles stand upright. This pole was nearly horizontal, and besides it carried no pulley or rope for attaching a flag.

*John Dewey, *How We Think*. New York: D. C. Heath & Co., 1910, pp. 69-70.

Dewey next tried to conceive of the pole as an ornament. But such ornaments do not appear on ferryboats or tugboats, where he had seen poles similar to the one he now perceived. Thus, he decided that the pole with the gilded ball was not an ornament.

His next hypothesis was that the pole was the antenna for a wireless receiver. Antennae, however, are usually placed on the highest part of the boat whereas this pole was mounted rather low. He therefore rejected the concept of a wireless antenna.

It next occurred to him that the pole might be a "guide pole" to help the pilot steer the boat. It was mounted so that the steersman could easily see it. From the pilot's location the pole would project some distance in front where it would point in the direction in which the boat was going. Since the pilot was stationed at the very front of the boat he would need some such guide. The fact that tugboats had similar poles and similar problems of steering supported the idea that the pole was a guide pole. Mr. Dewey therefore accepted the concept of the guide pole, concluding that his percept belonged to that category. He considered his problem solved, since he had related the pole with the gilded ball to similar poles and related this whole class to the guiding of ships.

If one analyzes this illustration he finds the now familiar three elements: percepts, concepts, and generalizations. The percepts are ideas representing individual things such as the white pole surmounted by a gilded ball, as well as a ferryboat on which the pole was slanting at a particular angle. Concepts are ideas referring to a class or group of things. The general idea brought to mind by the name *ferryboat,* the general idea represented by the word *tugboat,* the general ideas of flagpole and pilot are concepts. Generalizations in the illustration are found in the following: "Flagpoles stand upright." "Radio antennae are usually placed in the highest part of the boat." "Ornaments do not usually appear on ferryboats."

These elements of thinking are used in more complicated procedures called induction and deduction. We turn now to the problems of induction.

Chapter 2

INDUCTION AND THE SCIENTIFIC METHOD

We have found the elements of thinking to be percepts, concepts, and generalizations. Since these are subject to error they must be verified if truth is to be found. Such verification is the task of induction. Percepts are established, classified into concepts and classes of concepts from which suitable generalizations are derived. One of the main assumptions governing induction is that all the facts in the universe are related. Every fact is assumed to be consistent with every other fact in an orderly system to which they all belong. It is the determination of these facts, relationships, and laws that the inductive scientist seeks. Such a system, once completed, would be adequate to explain and solve most of the problems that men face.

ESTABLISHING FACTS

Facts of Personal Observation. A good deal of the time you will have to be your own "scientist." Much of your thinking will depend on your own observations, the people you listen to, the doctors and lawyers you select to advise you, and the ideas you accept or reject in your reading.

You carry the sole responsibility for the accuracy of your own observations. Since errors are frequent you should carefully check whatever you see or hear whenever you expect to think with the data. First, note your readiness to make the observation: Did you have a question in your mind when you saw this thing happen? Did the observation conform to your expectations or go contrary to it? If you were expecting nothing, were you ready to make the observation when you did, or were you interrupted in some other activity? Second, notice what other things took place at the same time: Were you able to give your undivided attention to the event, or was it incidental to various other events which you were observing? Were you alone at the time of the observation, or was someone with you? If someone was with you, did he have any influence on your observations? Did he make any suggestions, and if so, what were they? Did you measure any of the phenomena you saw? Were you careful in your measurements? Did you do any sampling—that is, did you make several observations at different times and places? Did you experiment in any way? In the third place, notice what incidents followed the event: Did you record your observations at the time, and were conditions good for making a careful recording? Is there any reason for you to prefer one belief rather than another?

Facts of Vicarious Experience. Much of everyone's information is learned from others. How are you to know whether you are reading or hearing the truth? Some of this information will be mistaken and must be discarded. Since you are unable to go back to the sources and examine the facts for yourself, you must examine the reliability of the intermediary. First, learn the nature of the observer: Is he ignorant or well-trained? Is he careful, cautious, and conscientious, or is he overemotional? Is the person dealing with his own field of knowledge, as when an engineer reports on engineering, or is it the statement of an engineer about the love life of the pigmies? In the second place, look for motivation: Is it possible that the observer was prejudiced or had an ax to grind? Is he a salesman or propagandist? Was the statement made in good faith? In the third place, note how many times the information has been transferred, since it tends to become more distorted with every transfer: Is this person reporting his own knowledge and experience or someone else's knowledge and experience? Did he hear this from someone who heard a second party relate it to a third? In the fourth place, check the time lag between the observation and the report. Caesar wrote his *Gallic Wars,* or the notes for the book, on the spot, and in consequence his account is usually considered accurate. Plutarch wrote his *Lives* about men, some of whom, like Lycurgus, had been dead a thousand years. Many of his statements, therefore, are not considered factual. Fifth, is the person who made the statement someone like Charles Darwin, who is long dead, or is he living? If alive, how recently were his observations made? Science repeats all questionable observations until the most skeptical person is satisfied. New instruments are continually being devised to improve observations. Many great authorities such as Aristotle, Newton, and Darwin have been found to be in error in individual instances, so it is always wise to look for recent support for statements of questionable or abstruse information.

If one is depending on the instructions given him by some professional person, such as a doctor or lawyer, he may examine this individual with further tests. (1) Is he a qualified person? Does he have a degree from a recognized university? Is he properly licensed? (2) Does he have the respect of associates in his own field, as indicated by membership in their societies? If a doctor, is he on the staff of a good hospital? Does he belong to the American Medical Association? Such information is readily available to those who ask. (3) Is this individual personally disinterested? Doctors seldom treat members of their own families. The United States Government, in appointing high officers, has been very careful to select men who are not in a position to benefit from their own advice. (4) Is this supposed authority willing to sign his name to his statements? In advertisements of medical and dental remedies, the statement "doctors recommend" is sometimes seen. Such endorsements are worthless since no one with an established reputation has been willing to give his name to the statement.

When one is not acquainted with the authors of the books and magazine articles he reads, he may apply some checks to the subject matter itself. (1) Is this material something that can be carefully scrutinized, or is it something like clairvoyance that is elusive and difficult to observe? (2) Is the information given in simple words, or is technical language used which must be interpreted? Are the statements confirmed by other writers? (4) Are the data consistent with everything that is already known? Since all the facts of the universe are thought to be consistent with each other, any inconsistency of alleged facts is considered suspicious.

Facts of Science. Wherever there has been science there have been attempts at careful observation. Aristotle, for instance, recorded the heartbeat of a chicken's embryo while it was still in the egg. After Aristotle the path of science was clouded for almost two thousand years. A few advances were made in Alexandria where the Arabs contributed their numerals, and in India where the symbol for zero was invented, The method of induction, however, was almost forgotten in the preoccupation of that time with the dogmas of religion.

Then Roger Bacon (1214-1294) reawakened an interest in experience. He declared that facts should not be accepted until they were verified. As a Franciscan monk, Roger Bacon gave a religious interpretation to the search for knowledge, declaring that its object was to know the Creator by the evidence of the external world. He called on scholars to break the bonds of custom by recognizing the indispensability of experience.

Although no immediate reform followed the work of Roger Bacon, he opened the way for the work of *Francis* Bacon, who lived in England over three hundred years later. Francis Bacon re-established the inductive method. Although not a major scientist he was, nevertheless, one of the most effective advocates of science who ever lived. Knowledge must begin with observation rather than with generalization, he believed, pointing out that "What in observation is loose and vague, is in information deceptive and treacherous."

Techniques of Observation. Careful, unbiased observation has been considered the essence of scientific knowledge ever since the time of Francis Bacon. This is true even though the variety and complexity of the facts that must be examined have fractured the method of observation into a great many techniques, from the controlled experiments of the laboratory to the repeated, instrumented observations of the distant stars in the sky.

All the various techniques of observation are alike in having the same two enemies, *authority* and *emotion*. Authority interferes with observation since the one who accepts the dictation of authority does not observe for himself. When the philosophers declared that all heavenly bodies moved in circles because the circle was the perfect form, there was very little careful observation of the movements of the stars. As science has grown, it has built its own formidable authority which has often prevented workers from finding what otherwise they might have found. The quantum theory, for instance, which contradicted previous scientific conclusions was opposed by many scientists for more than twenty years after it had been introduced. Pasteur had to brave powerful scientific opposition in proposing his discoveries with microorganisms. Wherever partially satisfactory theories are entrenched, new hypotheses are likely to have a difficult time.

Emotion is the enemy of observation, since the emotional observer does not view things clearly. Any excitement, such as fear, or enthusiasm, is likely to distort the view of the observer. Scientists are sometimes said to be "cold" because they train themselves to avoid emotionalism in their work. Before facts can be considered scientifically established they must run the gauntlet of skeptical examination.

Many scientists are even averse to careful, conscientious observation that is directed toward its own operations in the process called *introspection*. An example is putting salt on one's tongue and observing the taste. No one else can experience with you your taste of the salt. Nor can you repeat the experience of tasting salt for the first time. Introspection is a unique, unshared procedure and consequently is not trusted by skeptical scientists.

Science accumulates only shared experience. Whereas an artist takes pride in the unique, the scientist seeks the universal. A painting such as *The Last Supper* by Leonardo da Vinci derives much of its value from the fact that the perspective of the faces, as arranged by Leonardo, are strikingly different from those presented by any other painter. Artists do not like to paint identical pictures any more than women like to wear similar hats.

In science, on the other hand, the individual scientist is insignificant in contrast to the truth he finds. Truth, as contrasted to an artist's skill, is not individual but universal. When a million children are given a vaccine to prevent disease, each one of the inoculations is expected to have the same effect.

The basis of science, therefore, is the verified percept that has been compared with other percepts, its individual accidents eliminated, its generalized essence defined and raised to the level of a concept. Conceptual knowledge forms the defined, sharable information we call science.

CLASSIFICATION OF PERCEPTS, CONCEPTS, AND CLASSES

Classification. Classification gives significance to unrelated and consequently meaningless facts. It is one of the most fundamental processes carried on by the human mind. When a baby learns to recognize all the various "faces" presented by his mother—smiling, frowning, sad, tired, and laughing—and to distinguish his mother from all other people, he has completed a task in classification.

Without any formal instruction, as one grows up, he reduces

all the infinite variety of his environment to groups and sub-
groups. Any boy will identify a leaf from a tree without hesita-
tion. It is similar to, and different from, millions of other leaves.
If it were necessary to consider each leaf as an individual object
the mind would be left in absolute confusion. A man would spend
his whole life in examining leaves.

No matter which way a man turns, he finds the universe divided, classified, and grouped by this natural inclination of the
human mind.

The newspapers separate society, sports, and political news.
Books are divided into chapters; business and educational institutions into departments; the defenses of the country into Army,
Air Force, and Navy. People are grouped into families, clans, nations, and races. Everywhere we turn we find the mind classifying the objects of its environment. It is our way of reducing confusion to order and complexity to simplicity. Even poets classify,
as did Edgar Allan Poe in *The Bells:*

> Hear the sledges with their bells—
> > Silver bells!
> What a world of merriment their melody foretells!
> Hear the mellow wedding bells—
> > Golden bells!
> What a world of happiness their harmony foretells!
> Hear the loud alarum bells——
> > Brazen bells!
> What a tale of terror, now, their turbulency tells!
> Hear the tolling of the bells—
> > Iron bells!
> What a world of solemn thought their monody compels!

When philosophers began to examine what a man can know
and how he can know it, they discovered the essential nature of
classification. Most of the knowledge accumulated by the scientific method would have been lost had it not been possible to
store it away, assembled in orderly groups. We have, for instance,
a systematic group of facts, separated from all others, which we
call *physics*. Another large class of facts is called *chemistry*. Each
science is an orderly collection of information about some aspect
of the world. Any one can find, in an adequate library, any fact
that has been published. All scientifically verified facts have been
preserved in a form that permits them to be referred to in the
solution of any problem.

Lest the student reader overlook the fact, it should be noted that classification is one of the first aids to study in that it is the essential means of comprehending any assembly of information. Let the student examine the classification of facts before him and the reason for the particular grouping, and he will make a long stride toward the mastery of his subject.

The essence of classification is the similarity of a number of facts. This may be either a superficial similarity, as is found in an index, or a similarity in nature. The first type of classification is most useful in filing away information in libraries and business records where it can be found again, whereas the second type called natural classification is useful in understanding how facts are related.

There are three basic principles of natural classification: (1) The same principle of grouping should be used throughout one classification. (2) There should be no overlapping of classes or subclasses. (3) Every pertinent fact should have a specific place in the grouping.

Almost any group of facts can be classified in accordance with a number of different principles. Foods can be classified according to the amount of protein they contain, their cost, their availability in the local market, the amount of work required to prepare them for the table, or the personal preferences of the individual. Any one of these principles of classification is legitimate if it answers the purpose for which the classification is being made. To use all of them at once, or even two at the same time would, however, result in confusion.

But it is possible to subdivide a classification on a different principle from that of the original grouping. For instance, if foods were first classified according to their availability in a particular market, these groups might next be subdivided on some other principle, such as their nutritional value. Each particular classification, however, must be made on the basis of a single principle, known as the basis of classification.

The rule that facts should be grouped on the basis of one principle only, for a particular classification, is illusory in its simplicity and is sometimes abused. For instance, when numbers from one to seven are put in Class I, and numbers from eight to eleven are put in Class II, the error is made of using two principles of classification at the same time. The quality of being a number is one of the principles of selection, and quantity is the second. (Such distributions are made in statistics, with safe-guards known to statisticians, but distributions are not classes.) The error in classification is compounded when the individual members of the class are all described in terms of the average, or typical number. Deviating members, one to seven, of Class I, and eight to eleven, of Class II, would not be recognizable in terms of their averages. No one would identify a one or a seven because of its remarkable similarity to a four, or because they are so much like each other in quantity. It is as though one's temperature were always described as normal whether or not he had a fever.

This error is seldom made with numbers alone but it is fre-quently made when qualities other than numbers are represented. An example of such a distribution, used as a classification, is the one relating to extraversion and introversion. Human beings sometimes observe their own thought processes, an activity that is called introspection. Some people introspect more than others and an attempt has been made to classify people on the basis of how much time they spend in this activity. The subclasses are the introvert, who spends much time in introspection; the ambi-vert, who spends an average amount of time; and the extravert who spends little time. The classes are diagrammed below. There is obviously no real separation between the classes.

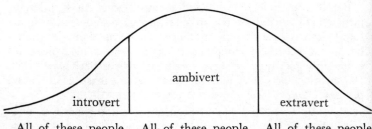

introvert	ambivert	extravert
All of these people spend much time in introspection	All of these people spend little time in introspection	All of these people spend an average amount of time in introspection

There are further examples of this error, which is relatively common. In psychology the description of various levels of intelligence was at one time assigned to a range of IQs. The various levels were:

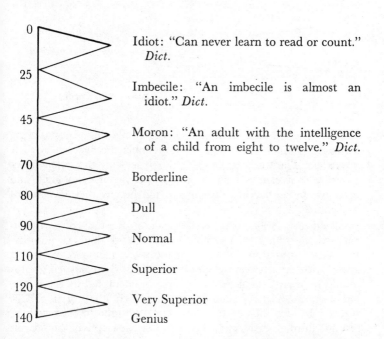

0	Idiot: "Can never learn to read or count." *Dict.*
25	Imbecile: "An imbecile is almost an idiot." *Dict.*
45	Moron: "An adult with the intelligence of a child from eight to twelve." *Dict.*
70	Borderline
80	Dull
90	Normal
110	Superior
120	Very Superior
140	Genius

Such classifications, even though they appear to clarify problems, are apt to make trouble. In some states, for instance, laws have required that morons who get into trouble be placed in institutions. This might mean that a person with an IQ of 69 be put in an institution for life, while one with an IQ of 71 be released. This problem, which has given many mental examiners trouble, is usually resolved now by a board of experts rather than determined by a particular IQ.

Another example of subclassifications being described in terms of their typical member is found in the honors given certain ranges of college students of *summa cum laude, magna cum laude,* and *cum laude.* In one university, for instance, the ranges used are these:

Student average

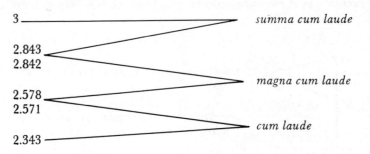

Many *summa cum laude* students resemble the nearest *magna cum laudes* much more than they resemble the average of their own class. The same principle holds true with the *cum laudes*. Just why universities would want to give courses in logic and then encourage careless thinking in the honors they give is not known.

Classifications should never be made on the basis of two principles at the same time, even though one of them is quantity. It is bad practice magnified to identify the members of such a group with the average person of that class. Systematized groups should be treated as such. Let people be identified by their IQs, but a range of them should not be named idiots. Let college students be identified by their numerical position in class, as first, second, third, fourth, etc., but a special description should not be attached to a range of students with different achievements. Although classification is a very useful tool, its misuse is not beneficial.

The second rule of classification forbids the overlapping of groups. If horses should be described as work horses, riding horses, and white horses, this error would be committed, since white horses may be either work horses or riding horses. Likewise, it would be erroneous to group science students as students of biology, students of physics, and students of science. Each category of the grouping should represent a distinct subclass.

The third rule of classification is that every item should have its specific place. A personal account book with a column for miscellaneous items illustrates this point. The difficulty with the miscellaneous column is that it is no classification at all, and that items put there are not really classified. One of the most complete classifications is the Periodic Table used in chemistry. Here all the elements have their places definitely determined, so therefore, there is no section for "miscellaneous elements." All substances in the Periodic Table are classified according to one principle: the nature of the atom, with particular regard to the number of its negative electrons and the positive charge of the nucleus.

Since there are no formal techniques for making classifications or determining into what groups to place individual items, less is said about this subject than its importance merits. The mind automatically groups and classifies many elements of experience. Science has set its stamp of approval on this process and has formalized it. Classified knowledge is in the right form to suggest hypotheses and definitions; it is ready for use.

ESTABLISHING GENERALIZATIONS

It is reasonable to suppose that there is some explanation for the similarity in the facts classified into one group. It is also reasonable to suppose that an action that is suitable as a response to one of the facts will be suitable to the others. When one formulates an explanation or rule for dealing with these closely related items, this statement is a generalization. Generalizing is one of the means at our disposal for simplifying life. All trees grow upward, all roots grow downward, all fire is hot, and all ice is cold. Like the mythical tailor who killed "seven at one blow," the man with a good, sound generalization can reduce a complex situation to a simple one.

Generalizations expressed without due care are often untenable. The two most common examples of this occur when a generalization is expressed without noting any exceptions, and when limited experience is crystallized into unacceptable conclusions. Examples of generalizing without noting exceptions are: "Familiarity breeds contempt," and "Ignorance is bliss." In generalizing from limited experience we find such statements as: "Teen-Agers have it too easy today"; "Early wed, early dead"; "A merry man is usually a fool." Many improper generalizations will be found where some one has taken a nonessential characteristic of some members of a group and assigned it to all of them. Such misleading generalizations are almost endless. "All Japanese are cunning"; "All Irishmen are flatterers"; "All Jews are aggressive"; "All negroes are ignorant"; "Every successful man will be found to have inherited money"; "Every beautiful woman is 'made-up'."

It is obvious that generalizations should be substantiated before use. Science recognizes this responsibility and verifies the generalizations it sponsors.

Hypotheses. An unproven generalization is a hypothesis. It is a preliminary assumption of some principle adopted to explain observed facts. A creative act is required in developing a hypothesis. As a tentative explanation it helps to guide observations to completion, suggesting a question here and a possibility there. As data are gathered, a hypothesis is either disproved and discarded, or accorded more status. The terms *speculation, hypothesis, theory,* and *law* form a progression according to the increasing adequacy of the evidence.

Since hypotheses are tentative, one of their main functions is to guide further observation. The aimlessness disappears from fact finding as soon as a hypothesis is proposed. One knows what to look for with his microscope or telescope, what to weigh or measure, or where to dig. Others may cooperate in the search; a whole army of scientists may go to work on the problem.

An example of a hypothesis that is directing a great deal of research is the one that "Cancer is caused by a virus." Millions of dollars are being spent, a large number of scientists are employed, with extensive equipment, to test this hypothesis.

Another example of a hypothesis that still directs a good deal of observation after years of activity relates to intelligence. It has been stated in different terms at different times, but today a good statement would be, "Education can increase intelligence." Lord Chesterfield (1694-1773) gave his son the best education that could be provided at that time in order to make a great man of him. He also wrote the boy a long series of advisory letters, which have become famous. But why his plans failed to work out he never understood. James Mill (1773-1836) thought intelligence could be produced, and, when his brilliant son John Stuart showed evidence of great accomplishment, he believed the credit was due, in large part, to the kind of education he had been given. Believing that he was developing intelligence rather than training it, Froebel (1782-1852) originated the kindergarten in Germany. In France, in 1798, a wild boy about fourteen-years old was found wandering in the woods.

The government took the boy in charge to make of him a test case. He was carefully tutored for three years with the avowed intention of educating him to be a philosopher. Although all efforts to educate the boy failed they led to the concept of the feeble-minded person as one who cannot be made intelligent by training. At about this time, the investigation led to the part played by heredity in producing high IQs. Other related questions were: Which is more important in intelligence, education or heredity? Are there methods of training such as "progressive education" or drill on fundamentals that lead to the greatest development? Is the mastery of mathematics more stimulating than the mastery of history? Is there a kind of heredity, such as "Nordic," Chinese, or Hebrew, that is more likely to produce high ability than others? These questions have stimulated a continuing stream of research all growing out of that simple original hypothesis, "Education can increase intelligence."

It will be observed that the hypothesis above is stated in the form of a declarative sentence. This is no indication of dogmatism since the purpose is merely to state the hypothesis clearly. A disproved hypothesis is discarded, but one that is supported by the evidence becomes, without any change in statement, a *theory,* and with still more evidence, a *principle,* then a *law.*

Hypotheses may be more or less adequate in explaining facts and in directing further observations. Four attributes will characterize a good hypothesis. In the first place, a hypothesis should be based on observations of fact which will permit it to be proven or disproven. The following statements, which cannot be tested, are not good hypotheses. "If the Roman Empire had not fallen, the civilization of the world would be centuries ahead today"; "The individual has an unconscious memory of the experiences of the human race"; The purpose of the universe is to provide an environment where man can reach his highest development." There is little or no value in stating a hypothesis if there is no way to test it.

In the second place, a good hypothesis should have sufficient significance to be worth investigating. There is no general interest in a speculation that deals with only one situation such as that an automobile has stalled because its gas tank has become empty. Of wider interest, but still limited appeal, is the hypothesis that the desert can be made an attractive residential area by building air-conditioned houses. Of a much higher level of significance, since it has much wider scope, is the theory that the direction of storms is controlled to some extent by the rotation of the earth.

A third criterion of a good hypothesis is that it leads to other hypotheses. The universe is an integrated system in which all knowledge is related to all other knowledge. In consequence, a good hypothesis may be expected to suggest further hypotheses. For example, a hypothesis about the rotation of the moon around the earth may lead to a similar hypothesis about the rotation of the planets around the sun. One of the most famous cases of one hypothesis leading to another is the Michelson-Morely Experiment. These men were testing some hypotheses concerning ether when they made certain discoveries concerning the speed of light. These discoveries, in turn, proved to be the spark for Einstein's Theory of Relatively, perhaps the most important theory in the history of science.

A further test of a hypothesis is that of simplicity, called "Ockham's razor" from William of Ockham. The assumption behind this rule is that nature always does things in the most simple, economical, and direct way possible. The best hypothesis, therefore, as to what nature is doing will be the simplest one capable of explaining the phenomenon in question. There are two aspects to this rule. It calls for the explanation that is the most economical in the number of propositions used in its statement, as well as the most economical in the number of exceptions that are found to its main thesis. The principle of simplicity does not call for easier explanations but for more elegant statements with unnecessary elements eliminated. As an example, the multiplication of five times five is usually explained simply as five times five rather than as five added to itself five times.

Methods of Verifying Hypotheses.   Hypotheses, as tentative generalizations, are more complex than might at first appear. A generalization, and therefore a hypothesis, is a terse description of some group of facts. This immediately brings up the question of whether the group of facts under consideration is complete and all of one kind. This must necessarily be verified.

Aristotle, one of the first to write on this topic, believed that the mind could determine intuitively from a few instances what would be true of all instances of one kind. It was not necessary to examine all cases, he thought, since the mind can distinguish the essential from the accidental characteristics of a class.

Francis Bacon, next to consider the problem, sought to eliminate negative cases and identify critical instances by separating the facts that had a consistent, inconsistent, or variable relation to the hypothesis. His methods, however, are too mechanical and complex for use.

It was left for John Stuart Mill (1806-1873) to originate the first practical methods for testing hypotheses. Mill looked for verification in unvaried repetition of instances under similar circumstances. Such repetition requires a fixed order of precedence in time, which is Mill's definition of cause and effect. To modern scientists, Mill appears a little naïve in his assumption that whatever he found true of John, Henry, Frank, and William, is true of all mankind. Today it is believed that such groups are never completed and that mankind may someday show an unexpected variation. However, from a practical point of view, Mill's methods have been of great value. Rather than naming the groups themselves, he named the techniques by which he assembled his groups. Prediction is based on laws or hypotheses, which, in turn, are the result of the "repetition of instances." Such repeated instances are analyzed for consistency.

Mill's Methods. Mill's methods are techniques for arranging facts in order to examine their repetitions. The causes and effects sought may need to be verified by application, but many problems have been solved by the use of these five methods alone: (1) the method of agreement; (2) the method of difference; (3) the joint method of agreement and difference; (4) the method of concomitant variation; and (5) the method of residues.

The Method of Agreement. Mill's method of agreement indicates that if a number of instances of a phenomenon have only one thing in common the common element must be related as cause or effect. When the method of agreement is diagrammed, as below, the circles indicate instances where the phenomenon

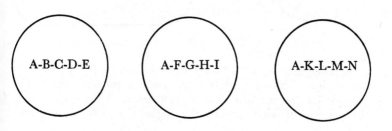

occurs. The different letters indicate the different factors that may be present in these situations. But one factor, in this case the letter A, is always present.

An illustration of the method of agreement is found in the case of "Typhoid Mary." This Mary was a servant girl living on Staten Island, New York. She had the misfortune of losing a number of jobs because someone in the families for whom she worked developed typhoid fever, so that a nurse was needed rather than kitchen help. Her bad luck continued, as more of her employers had typhoid fever. Finally, it became apparent that the only uniform factor in all these families that had suffered from the fever was "Typhoid Mary." Wherever she worked, it appeared, someone developed typhoid fever. It was finally determined that Mary was a carrier of the disease, even though she was not subject to it herself. The Board of Health of New York City put Mary in an institution, where, except for one brief interval, she remained for the rest of her life.

The Method of Difference. The essence of the method of difference is the demonstration that different results occur in situations that are identical except for one factor. If variable results occur in several instances that are identical except for one element, the variable element must be related, as cause or effect, to the variable results. The method can be diagrammed as follows, in which F is the cause.

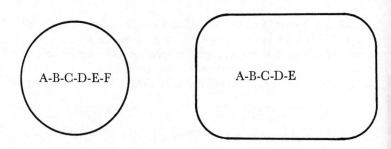

A person may apply the method of difference, for example, if the engine of his automobile is not working properly. He might compare the engine with that of another car of the same make. By noticing in what manner the engine that was not working properly differed from the one that was working properly, he would determine the reason for the first engine's failure.

The Joint Method of Agreement and Difference. Here we find circumstances of the "now you have it—now you don't," variety. If the situations that produce a particular result also have a particular element, and the situations that do not produce the result lack also that particular element, then the element present in the first group and lacking in the second is the cause of the phenomenon in question. A simple illustration is the case of a number of persons during an epidemic, some of whom are inoculated with a vaccine and some of whom are not. It may then be found that, regardless of living conditions or contact with sick persons, those persons vaccinated did not catch the disease and the others did. The method can be diagrammed as follows, V standing for Vaccinated and U for Unvaccinated.

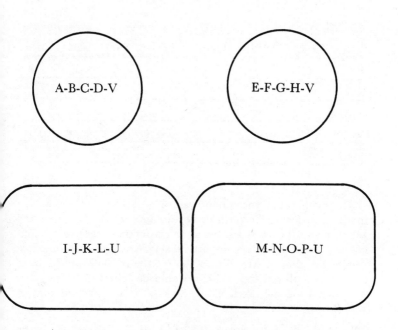

The Method of Concomitant Variations. Circumstance are concomitant when they are conjoined or accompany each other.

The method of concomitant variations seeks causes and effects wherever phenomenon vary together. This method can be illustrated by a graph as given below, showing how a particular young man's rising time varies with his time for going to bed.

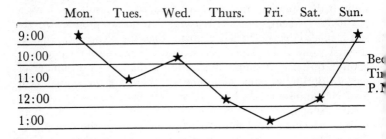

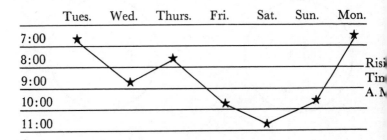

The method of concomitant variations is imperfect, requiring that its conclusions be verified. For instance, both Mr. Jones and Mr. Brown, who work for the same corporation, receive a bonus in good years but none in bad years. Mr. Jones' income tax varies with that of Mr. Brown; in good years both are high, in bad years both are low. Still, it would be improper to say that Mr. Jones' income tax is either a cause or an effect of that of Mr. Brown.

The Method of Residues. The fifth of Mill's methods is the method of residues. Here a cause is sought by eliminating one possibility after another, until finally, only the cause is left. We may take, as an example, a complicated machine with four knobs. A curious person may want to determine which of the knobs controls the speed. If he discovers that three of the knobs produce other effects, he can therefore assume that the fourth knob controls the speed. (For some situations this illustration is oversimplified. In finding the cause of the common cold, the number of "knobs" or possible causes in unknown.) In such cases, experiment must remove one suspected cause after another until the true "residue" is reached. This method, with the four knobs, can be diagrammed as follows, where A-B-C-D (knobs) are causes and W-X-Y-Z are effects.

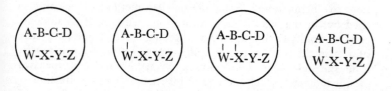

The Experimental Method. Since Mill, there has been increased doubt that the uniformities of nature can all be readily separated from its accidents. But science makes never-ending efforts to do so and has refined the experimental, clinical, and survey methods for this purpose.

There are many cases in which it is very difficult to isolate a particular fact for examination. These situations have required the scientist to exert the greatest ingenuity. For this reason, the experimental method has been developed to permit accurate observation in all sorts of confusing situations. This method can be used only where certain decisive factors can be held constant or changed at will. Its rules, reduced to the simplest form, require that all the significant factors in the experiment be controlled, except the phenomenon whose nature is the center of interest. Only two factors should be allowed to vary; the force that is acting on the phenomenon under observation is varied in a controlled manner, while the factor that is being observed varies as its nature requires. For instance, in an experiment to determine the influence of high altitudes on airplane pilots, all factors must be controlled except the behavior of the pilots examined. The altitudes flown will be varied in a predetermined manner. The changing behavior of the pilots under the conditions of the varied altitudes is the information sought.

Control of significant factors is sometimes obtained by the use of a "control group." In the experiment above, a control group of pilots might fly similar airplanes under similar conditions of wind, temperature, speed, and hours in the air as those experienced by the test group, but with altitude held constant.

Control groups are used in many fields of investigation. A new drug, for instance, is tested by selecting two groups of patients who are as nearly alike as possible. One group is given the new drug and the other—the control group—is not given it, though a placebo, or sugar pill, may be administered if psychological reactions are being tested. Sometimes a new method of teaching is tried out in this way. The control group, composed of students equal in ability to the experimental group, is taught the particular subject in the usual way, while the experimental group is taught it in the new way. The comparative achievement of the two groups indicates which method of instruction is more effective.

Since the experimental method of observation has been adapted to many specialized fields it is impossible to describe all of the adaptations here. Research workers are always instructed during their training in the particular techniques of experimentation needed in their area. Among scientific problems to be solved by special applications of the experimental method are those faced by the physicist and the chemist who must operate the atom smasher to break down the atoms into their components.

Atom smashing is so expensive that no nuclear physicist can assemble his own equipment to make his own observations. In earlier centuries private observation in physics was possible, but this is becoming rare. Today, on some problems at least, millions of dollars must be spent before the first observation can be made. Two devices known at the present time for reducing the atom are cosmic rays and gigantic machines such as cyclotrons and betatrons. Working with cosmic rays requires either transporting complex equipment up high mountains or the launching of high-flying rockets and satellites. To build atom smashers requires millions of dollars and a small army of men is needed to operate them. The Los Alamos laboratory, located in the Jemez Mountains of New Mexico, for example, is surrounded by a small city of workers.

Psychologists face very different problems in which factors like the motivating forces for an action cannot be physically separated by any technique, but must be separated indirectly by statistical analysis and control groups. The physiologist faces still different problems, such as those posed by the phenomena of cancer. Men cannot be used as experimental "guinea pigs" in cases where they might be seriously harmed. So another and supposedly similar species is used for observation in cancer experiments. Here further verification is needed to make sure that the conclusions reached for the animals will hold also for men. In a recent experiment on cancer, cigarettes were smoked by machine. The tars set free by this machine were painted, three times a week, on the shaved skins of mice of a particular strain. More than half of these mice developed cancer within a year, at the location of the painting. But when an attempt was made to transfer this finding to support the conclusion that cigarette smoking produces cancer of the lungs in humans, quick objections were raised. The cancer might have been due to the strains of mice used, as some strains of mice are more susceptible to cancer than others. Perhaps the cancer resulted from the frequent small abrasions due to the repeated shaving. The cancers may have come not from the tobacco tars but from the solvent used in producing a liquid that could be painted on the mice. In consequence of these criticisms the experiment was considered suggestive but not conclusive.

The Clinical Method. In the clinical method all the factors of a complex situation are observed intact so there is no need to transfer conclusions as from mice to men. The skill and wisdom of the observer are depended upon as he varies and emphasizes different factors which he wishes to evaluate. Many of the clinical observations of Sigmund Freud, for instance, dealt with the motivation of people. He constructed hypotheses of instinctive forces, of repression, of the ambivalence of hate and love. Both his observations and his conclusions relate directly to his patients. Some of his conclusions have been widely accepted, but others have not.

The clinical observer may depend upon the aid of instruments or tests. One device used in studying motivation is to present to the subject an ambiguous design, such as an ink blot, or a slightly "slanted" picture, such as that of a young man gazing into the distance as he stands on a sidewalk with a broom in his hand. The subject is told to tell a story about the picture. One subject might see the young man with the broom as daydreaming about his future and planning how he can become a successful executive. Another person might see him as disappointed at having to sweep the sidewalk at a time when his companions have gone to the beach for a gay outing. In these stories the psychologist hunts for the dominating motivation of the narrator.

The family physician seeking the cause of illness is the most common example of the operation of clinical techniques. The doctor asks questions and watches the results closely as he tries out his medicines. For him each patient is a new problem.

Various methods may be used simultaneously on the same problem. In consequence, we will find that the probability of a relationship between cigarette smoking and cancer has been studied by the clinician as well as by the experimentalist. The clinician compares the smoking-habits of those who develop cancer with those who do not. This method is more open to the influence of intangibles than is the experimental method. In England, a number of physicians have said they feel positive that cigarette smoking does cause cancer. Such opinions given as the result of clinical observations are not considered conclusive unless supported by massive clinical evidence.

The Survey Method.   The survey method, like the clinical method, observes the phenomenon without taking it apart or experimenting. The best illustration of the survey method at work is the surveyor, measuring land and describing carefully the objects he finds there. The astronomer uses the survey method in watching the heavens through his telescope, plotting the stars and determining their movements. The geologist depends upon survey techniques in searching the earth for minrals and studying the rock formations of different areas. Most of the knowledge we have of the calendar, of navigation, and of the resources of the earth, is the contribution of surveys. Knowledge of hurricanes, cyclones, floods, erosion, and many other such phenomena is acquired by the survey method.

Surveys may be made to examine the same problems that are observed by clinical and experimental methods. The effects of cigarette smoking have been examined by all the methods available. Surveys indicate that lung cancer has increased more or less concomitantly with the increase in the sale of cigarettes. Men, who smoke more than women, suffer in greater proportion from lung cancer. Smokers in the army, compared with nonsmokers in the same age groups, show greater mortality from cancer. This is very probably significant, but it is not conclusive. (Smog has increased too, and other unrecognized factors may have increased as well, any one of which might be the cause of cancer.)

Summary. Generalizations are established after serving as hypotheses which are thoroughly tested. Science does not accept its generalizations easily or take them lightly. We have seen in Mill's methods as well as in the experimental, the clinical, and the survey method how carefully facts are tested. Classifications are examined with equal care, and once generalizations are made they are tested further. If a serious flaw is found in a scientific generalization, it is promptly abandoned. Over the years, however, a great many sound generalizations have been established.

Everyone has heard of the Theory of Relativity and the Law of Gravitation. There are many other scientific generalizations which, though not so far reaching as these, are part of our common knowledge. A few illustrations are:

(1) Living organisms are composed of cells; (2) The lungs excrete wastes formed by oxidation; (3) Emotion can interfere with clear thinking; (4) All living things must adapt themselves to their environment or perish; (5) The sun is the chief source of energy for all plants and animals.

There is today an enormous amount of verified knowledge stored in our books and libraries. But in this state it is somewhat like the gold bullion stored under the ground at Fort Knox, Kentucky. To be applied to the solution of problems this knowledge must be coined and used in reasoning.

Chapter 3

PROBABILITY AND STATISTICS

THE NATURE OF PROBABILITY

The determination of probabilities by the use of statistics is an adjunct to induction not planned by Aristotle. Induction, as we have seen, deals with the determination of facts, classes and generalizations. Aristotle, who was interested only in separable discrete facts that can be counted, left to intuition the satisfactory completion of classes. Having examined a few chickens' eggs he was ready to assume that the eggs of all chickens would be like the few. No statistics were needed for this type of classification. But facts are not always separate and discrete. Prior to World War I, about seventeen percent of United States citizens were said to have German ancestry. Kaiser Wilhelm assumed that because of this, the United States would never fight Germany, and so began the U-boat warfare. But the facts here are harder to determine than might at first appear. The German heredity of U. S. citizens is not of uniform degree. It is not true that "this one is German and that one is not," but rather one person's heredity is wholly German, another's is a half, one a third, and one a sixteenth. The assumption that the Americans would not fight was only a probability which was underestimated by the Kaiser.

Various circumstances, from pure chance to high probability, are involved in many fact finding ventures. To deal with these complex situations where classifications cannot be easily made or completed, three kinds of probability theory have been devised: the mathematical theory, the qualitative theory, and the frequency theory. Statistics is the branch of knowledge by which applications of the last two theories are made.

The Mathematical Theory.   Pierre de Laplace (1749-1827), French mathematician and astronomer, originated the mathematical theory in response to the questions of one of his friends who was interested in gambling. Rather than dealing with facts this theory explains reasonable expectations in chance situations. For instance, if one throws a die, the probability is one-sixth that any one face will fall upright, but, which face it will be cannot be told. The primary value of the mathematical theory is, as it was with Laplace's gambling friends, to determine reasonable expectations in various chance situations. It is said that a person who plays bridge in accordance with the mathematical probabilities will improve his game. Provided there is no manipulation or interference with chance, a knowledge of the probabilities will also help a gambler to understand his chances of winning. As we shall see, however, chance seldom has full sway.

Three conditions rule mathematical probability: the desired result looked for must be known, as in "heads I win"; the total number of alternatives must be known, as in "heads or tails"; and the alternatives must be equally probable, as in a case where the penny is perfectly balanced and tossed so that either heads or tails is equally possible. Under these circumstances, the mathematical probability of an occurrence is the number of favorable ways divided by the total number of possible ways. The odds, which are different from the mathematical probabilities, are the favorable ways divided by the unfavorable ways. The mathematical probability of heads coming up in a penny toss are one in two, while the odds are one to one, or fifty-fifty, in common terms. The calculations become more complex with dice and cards. The chance that a particular card will come up in bridge is one in fifty-two, or that an ace of any suit will come up is four in fifty-two, or one in thirteen.

Mathematical probabilities relate also to both compound independent and compound dependent situations. An example of a compound independent instance is the probability of getting two fives in two throws of dice. Getting one five in no way affects the chances of getting a second five. The compound probability is found by multiplying the independent probabilities by each other. Dependent probabilities are illustrated by the chances of drawing apples from a bag containing a given number of apples and oranges. Every time an apple or orange is drawn the probabilities change for the remainder. With this circumstance noted, the mathematical rule is the same as with independent compound cases. If there are six oranges and six apples in the bag, the chances of drawing two apples in the two tries are 6/12 for the first, and 5/11 for the second, or 6/12 times 5/11 for the two trials, which is 5/22.

The difficulty of finding pennies, dice, or cards that faithfully obey the laws of chance is illustrated in the following instance. Two college boys went to Las Vegas, Nevada, to make their fortunes based on the following assumptions: No real object, die, card, or piece of furniture is perfect; in consequence, roulette wheels cannot be perfect. If the defect in a roulette wheel can be found, a person who bets to take advantage of this defect should make substantial winnings. The boys watched a particular roulette wheel for thousands of spinnings, recording each stop. They found that it did stop, as they had predicted, more often on some numbers than on others. Betting on these numbers the boys began to make money. If they could have continued unobserved, they might have made more money. But their secret slipped out. The newspapers wrote an amusing story about the incident, the roulette wheel was rebalanced, and the boys were left no recourse but to look for more remunerative "employment."

Another case deals with horse-racing. A statistician adopted the assumption that most people who bet on the horses do so on the basis of hunches, without any method to guide them. A statistician who places his bets on mathematical probabilities determined by the records of the various horses should be able to make gambling a business and harvest a fortune. Horses of the optimum age win more races than old ones or very young ones. Certain horses and certain jockeys have better records than other horses and other jockeys. The weight carried is also an important factor since heavy weights are a handicap. Combining such factors into a system was a simple statistical task. The betting technique used was to place bets to offset one another in such a way that it was impossible to win or lose a great deal at one time. The man aimed at about 40 per cent interest on his money.

At the end of each year the statistician balanced his books and made out a report, as was demanded by his scientific training. One year the report read, "I lost forty dollars this year, but worked out a much better integration of my system." The next year the report read, "I earned a hundred-and-fifty dollars this year. I begin to feel certain of my method." The following year the statement was, "Only ten dollars ahead this year. I can't figure out what is wrong." The experiment continued for ten years.

The statistician finally determined to his own satisfaction that although he could examine the records of the horses and determine the probabilities of winning for each one, he had no way of determining manipulation. Horses are not always run to win, and many other possibilities of human interference with racing probabilities can annul a betting system. In brief, mathematical probability refers to theoretical situations rather than to actual ones. Understanding the theory prevents one from taking foolish chances in gambling but does not enable him to make any great gains, unless his opponent is foolish. Few games are purely chance, since skill, the imperfection of equipment, and the willful manipulation of circumstances interfere with this possibility. Gambling houses and race tracks, of course, depend not on probability for their income, but on a percentage of all the business done.

The Theory of Games. The mathematical theory of probability originated by Laplace relates to pure chance and is unable to deal with manipulation or the conflicting interests of the participants. Recently, a mathematical method called Game Theory has been developed that does examine aspects controlled by the participants. It has been worked out on models that resemble games such as poker and bridge, but its applications, so far, have been to neither parlor games nor gambling but to the problems of business, politics, and war. Game theory is designed to examine a situation in which there is incomplete information, conflicting interests, the interaction of free decision, and chance.

The "games" are classified on the basis of three different principles. The first of these depends upon interest and conflict. There are situations of only one interest, without conflict, as in solitaire. Other situations have two interests so that if one participant gains, the other loses. Again there are situations in which plural interests operate.

The second principle of classifying the "games" relates to the possible choices included. The game is rid of identifying elements, such as cards or poker chips, generalizing it, so that strategies of choice in the particular game can be determined. This permits the writing of a complete set of advance instructions giving a definite response for every possible choice which the player may have to make, whether these choices are presented by chance or by the acts of other players.

The third method of classification depends upon whether the game is finite, with a limited number of strategies, or whether it is infinite—usually a mathematical construct—as when the normal number of poker hands is replaced by a continuum of numbers.

By classifying the model games according to these three principles, strategic likenesses and differences are emphasized. Since it is a new method, recently developed by mathematicians, Game Theory has not been fully explored. One kind of situation that game theory will some day clarify is a political convention. In such a convention there are several candidates, each with a personal following. The "game" for each candidate is to secure the nomination by forming coalitions with other groups while preventing coalitions being formed against him. A certain "price" in terms of patronage is offered or withheld in arranging these coalitions. The mathematics of Game Theory should plan all probable decisions before the convention so that the candidate would know exactly what to do under all circumstances.

The Qualitative Theory. Qualitative probability depends upon the fact that a hypothesis is more firmly established every time it is substantiated by experience. A good example of this principle is Einstein's Theory of Relativity. After Einstein had derived his theory mathematically, the experimental physicists went to work with various devices to verify or disprove it. Every situation which substantiated the theory helped to verify it. Had it failed to work, the theory would have been discarded, even though parts of it might have been used in evolving some new theory. Qualitative probability, then, concerns the degree of certainty accorded to a particular hypothesis.

Qualitative probability also relates to the judgments of everyday life that are based, often not very analytically, on past experience. "Ben will probably be on time, because he nearly always is on time"; "I doubt if Frank will have an automobile accident, because he is driving his new car which he will not want to damage." Some qualitative probabilities are based on analogy. "It will probably rain. The last time we had a heavy rain, the clouds looked just as they do now." These probability judgments of everyday life must frequently be examined or they will lead to many errors.

The Frequency Theory. The English mathematician John

Venn, who, as we shall see in the next chapter, devised visual aids to deduction was one of the originators of the frequency theory of probability. Life expectancy and insurance premiums are now calculated by the use of this theory. A man's automobile premiums are based upon his fraction of the expense of the accidents that actually happen to the members of his insured group. If accidents increase his insurance costs go up; if accidents can be reduced his insurance costs come down. If he can qualify for insurance with some preferred group, such as "AAA Honor Drivers," he may secure his insurance at comparatively low rates.

The frequency theory depends upon the repetitions within a particular group. Suppose a man decides to buy an annuity for the remainder of his life. The insurance company might offer him such alternatives as these: three hundred dollars a month for the rest of his life, with payment to his heirs of his remaining capital should he die before all his capital is consumed; or three hundred and fifty dollars a month for the rest of his life, without the return of any of his capital even if he should die the following day. Assume the following conditions: the life expectancy of the average man of his age is twenty years. His health is better than average and he is employed at work suitable to his age. Both of these factors should aid him in living longer than his normal life expectancy. With the second alternative given above of three hundred and fifty dollars per month, he will recover all his capital if he merely lives out the average expectancy of his class, whereas, if he lives beyond it as he may well do, he will gain fifty dollars a month for the rest of his life.

All of the known probabilities relate to the average man of his class. This man may die tomorrow, even though he is favored by all the expectations given above. With the data described, however, he is able to make his decision with reasonable confidence.

STATISTICS

Statistics is that branch of mathematics which evaluates groups, or frequencies of data, that are not homogeneous. The functions of statistics are, in general, those of induction in situations where simple classification of homogeneous groups cannot be used. That is, statisticians determine facts by description as well as by measuring relationships in compound data without separating the elements. An example of statistical description is the statement of the millions of dollars needed for this or that specific project in the United States Budget. The application of statistical generalization is well-known to the average person through the proportion of his income on which he is expected to pay taxes.

It is said that statistics was born of mathematics when Galileo explained to some of his friends what they might expect in throwing dice. In the same century, and with the same motivation, statistics grew up under the tutelege of Laplace, when he devised the mathematical theory of probability. In the following centuries its applications widened, and it received contributions from many able mathematicians such as Gauss, Galton, and Pearson. We find statistics used everywhere in the modern world. Before a compact car is put on the market or a new helicopter is built, statistical evidence is sought that the article is wanted. Votes are counted to establish the popularity of entertainers while meters that register the quantity of the applause given them determine the size of their salaries. Statisticians inform politicians where their wavering followers need support. Military men use statistics to solve logistic problems.

Statistics are more complicated than simple classifications of homogenous groups, consequently they occupy an area where mistakes are easily made. Frequently too, statistics are advanced by pressure groups, who, innocently or intentionally, present facts in a biased manner. It has frequently been published, for instance, that there are more hospital beds occupied by the mentally disturbed than by people with all other illnesses combined. The statement has the worthy aim of arousing interest in mental hygiene. Its perpetrators, with their consciences fortified by their good intentions, however, do not point out that they mean "bed hours." There are not so many mental patients as the statement would imply; it is merely that a mental patient usually occupies his bed longer than other patients. This sort of manipulation of data favoring a particular objective goes on all of the time.

The individual does well to remember when he reads statistical information in the newspapers, the magazines, or company advertisements that the information has probably been given out with a purpose. Sometimes the agent is an honest person carried away by his own enthusiasms; sometimes he intentionally attempts to mislead; sometimes his presentation is objective and competent. But the reader is always responsible for what he believes. He can usually protect himself by applying elementary statistical knowledge such as is given here in the following pages: Is the sample sound? Have measures been used in obtaining the data? What is the central tendency of the data? What the range, the reliability, and the correlation with other things?

The Nature of the Units. The first task of statisticians is to gather information. This information must be objective rather than subjective. During the war there was a rumor among the American troups that Germany had developed a chemical antidote to fatigue. Each German soldier was said to carry a small kit containing this antidote which he could inject into his blood stream whenever he began to feel tired. The rumored result was that every German soldier was always miraculously fresh and ready to fight. But when this subjective information was checked objectively by searching and questioning captured Germans, the fatigue kits were found to be a fiction. After every disaster such as flood, earthquake or tornado exaggerated generalities are apt to be given out. The first reports often indicate that "hundreds are killed, thousands homeless," when later an actual listing shows "ten killed and eighty-five homes destroyed." The statistician always must begin his work by changing general figures into specific instances.

Sometimes, when units are not properly established, even counting can be misleading. Joe and Frank, interested in automobiles, own four cars each. But Joe buys old cars at the junk yard to rebuild them, while Frank buys sports cars to race them. Mr. Winters and Mr. Southern both own horse ranches stocked with a hundred horses each. But Mr. Winter's horses are work horses worth about two-hundred dollars each, while Mr. Southern's horses are race horses worth about two-thousand dollars each. Two cattle ranches are stocked with the same number of animals, but on one ranch they have native cattle, on the other thoroughbred stock. Things with the same name often differ in quality, and this difference must be recorded in the statistician's accounting.

Measuring units, bearing the same name, should also have a constant value under different circumstances. For instance, in educational achievement, we find four boys all graded "B" in mathematics. One came from a rural school, one from a parochial school, one from a big city public school, and one from a select private academy. It is very unlikely that their uniform grade of "B" indicates an equal uniformity of accomplishment.

Measures have another desirable attribute when they can be added or multiplied. For instance, a boy who weighs 180 pounds weighs twice as much as one weighing 90 pounds, and three times as much as one weighing 60 pounds. This uniformity is not true of the system of progressively numbered class intervals used in measuring the intelligence quotient. The I.Q. is competitively determined at each level, consequently it is not known that a boy with an I.Q. of 180 is twice as bright as one with an I.Q. of 90, or three times as bright as one with 60. The quantitative relationship of various I.Qs cannot be determined from the illusory numbers attached to them. This defect in the measure can lead to misunderstanding and error.

When different measures are taken of the same thing, as of height and weight, it is desirable that these measures do not overlap in an undetermined way. This is not always achieved in measuring the abilities of people. For instance, there are IQ tests, intelligence tests that are not IQ tests, scholastic aptitude tests, and achievement tests, none of which has clear relationships to each other. Theoretically, the relationships are comprehensible. IQs, for example, represent inherited ability. General intelligence tests represent a preponderance of inherited ability over acquired ability, with norms that are usually taken from some limited group, such as "5000 college students who have taken this test." Scholastic aptitude represents inherited ability subdivided and related to academic subjects. Finally, achievement tests represent the academic work a person can actually do. But practically, it is almost impossible to make the measures correspond to their definitions. Inherited ability can be measured only through the use of learned responses, and it is probable that limited test situations, given under the pressure of time, favor people with certain inherited characteristics. When used by experts who know what they are doing these measures are useful, but when interpreted by those involved they often give trouble. Here, for instance, is a boy with an I.Q. of 135, an intelligence score of 161, a scholastic aptitude score that puts him in the upper 5 per cent of those students who have been tested throughout the United States, and a school achievement that is so low that he is barely able to remain in school. His parents, feeling that they have endowed him with a high I.Q., go to sleep wondering what is wrong with the environment today. His teacher, worried at the variance of inheritance with achievement, stays awake trying to determine whether the difficulty is with her methods or with modern education. The boy himself, confident that he has "the ability," does not bother about his actual grades since, he says, "they don't mean anything anyway," and consequently goes his carefree way, failing to learn the things he will need later.

The clearly defined units required by thinking are often established by measurement. Some measurements are remarkably accurate and some are imperfect. The effort is to provide objective, discrete, countable units, that represent constant and clearly defined values.

Percentages. Less real money is needed to give a man a 10 per cent increase when he is earning sixty-dollars a week than when he is already earning six-hundred dollars a week. In the first place he would receive six dollars and in the second case sixty dollars. The immense difference in the same percentage when figured from a base of ten, one hundred, five hundred, or five hundred million, makes it possible to do considerable manipulation with percentages.

For political purposes, the growth of the United States has frequently been compared on a percentage basis with that of the industrially younger and less developed communistic Russia. The result is necessarily inaccurate.

A second somewhat common situation often occurs in the beginning of a business recession when the loss of business is calculated in terms of the previous month or previous year. This gives the calculation a relatively high base, and the loss in business may appear deceptively low until there is an accumulation of losses. When business picks up, it may be announced as a percentage increase of what it was the previous month or at its low point. An automobile company recently published jubilantly that its sales for March were 35 per cent higher than the sales for February, compounding misrepresentation with error since relatively few cars are ever sold in February, while the upturn seemed unduly promising because of the low base used in calculating the increase. Perhaps the concession to optimism and business confidence justified the misuse of the statistics.

It is sometimes helpful to turn the percentages into the actual quantities they represent, and vice versa, when a thorough understanding is sought.

Sampling. Although the first thing usually done in statistical work is to count and measure it is sometimes impossible to count all the cases. The particular items inspected, however, must be typical of the whole group since the ultimate aim here, as in other inductive procedures, is to discover underlying uniformities that may be described by hypotheses, theories, or laws. To have every instance properly represented it is necessary to avoid a biased selection. This often happens when the observer attempts to support some favored hypothesis which he brings to the work. A famous case of biased observation is phrenology, the effort to determine human character by the bumps on the head. This so-called science originated in France at the time of Napoleon, spread through Europe and America, and lasted till about the time of Ralph Waldo Emerson who refused to recommend the career laid out for a boy as determined by the shape of his head. The unreasonableness which Emerson found in phrenology was determined, at about this time, to be due to selecting cases for observation that supported a theory. It was asserted, for instance, that broad-headed people were fighters. This conclusion was supported by pointing out that Alexander the Great, Caesar, Hannibal, and Napoleon all had had broad heads. But when this conclusion was tested by measuring the heads of a sampling of the general population it appeared that "broad-heads were not more apt to fight than long-heads." Thus, proper sampling exposed one of the major errors of phrenology even before modern science rejected it completely.

A similar theory, proposed after insufficient sampling, is that indicating there is a criminal type of person who can be differentiated from normal people by his physical characteristics. Cesare Lombroso (1836-1909), professor of forensic medicine and psychiatry at Turin, Italy, and the first criminologist of modern times, examined the skulls, skin, bones, hair, and eyes, of many criminals and found them characteristic of man at an earlier and more primitive stage of development. Had he examined the same characteristics, as has been done since, in a random sampling of normal people, he would have found that many of them had the same physical characteristics without being criminals.

Recent experience with marketing and political polls has greatly improved the knowledge of sampling. The total population for which it stands must be accurately represented by a sample. If a group is homogeneous, very little sampling is required. The examination of one piece of pure gold is enough to describe all pieces of pure gold. But as a group loses its uniformity, the sampling must be sure to represent all the irregularities in proportion to their number.

A simple random, or chance, sampling eliminates subjective bias and the attempt to support a particular hypothesis, but takes no account of irregularities in the group. Housewives usually seek a random sampling, which improves with the number of items examined, when they buy apples by the basket. They often remove some of the top apples in the attempt to look at apples scattered at random through the whole basket. An insufficient sampling may be misleading. When polio inoculations were first used, one community divided its children into a test group and a control group. The test group was inoculated, and not a single one of its members developed polio! But soon it was noticed that neither did a single member of the control group. Finally, it was noted that even combining the two groups did not give a sample large enough to be significant. The expectation of polio for the combined group, without inoculation, was only two cases.

When a population is composed of mixed elements, it is necessary to sample each element in proper proportion. For instance, in polling the American people to predict a presidential election, it is necessary to sample by age, geographical areas, economic status, political party, and other factors that may be important at the time. Sometimes it is assumed that a subgroup, once established, will continue for years unchanged; but this is not always true, since proportions of older or younger people may increase, the number of farmers or those raising horses may decrease, and new cities may appear or become ghosts in certain geographical areas.

When the sampling is made for some particular purpose,

all aspects of this interest must be represented. For instance, a poll taken during the depression to determine the financial condition of the people must break down economic status in some detail. One such poll represented the population as 6 per cent wealthy, 23 per cent upper middle, 41 per cent lower middle, 30 per cent poor, with negroes in a separate group. Today, in most areas, the negro group would require sub-division.

Proper sampling is a major requirement of statistical thinking. Whenever a person says, "I'm sure I'm right, and I can find the evidence to prove it," he is in danger of falling into the error of observing only selected cases.

Distribution.   After facts of a kind have been gathered and measured it is desirable to put them in order. The first step, usually, is to determine the highest and lowest measure as well as the range between them. If one were measuring the head size of soldiers, for instance, preparatory to buying their hats, the range would be approximately from $6\frac{3}{8}$ to $7\frac{7}{8}$. The next thing is to break down this range into a suitable number of frequency steps. From ten to twenty steps is usually considered a manageable number, although the uniformity of each step must be considered. In the case, for example, of hats purchased for the army this matter is easily solved in terms of the sizes regularly manufactured, which determines that there will be thirteen classifications of hats, as given a little later on.

A visual means of charting these frequencies was originated by the famous French philosopher René Descartes, whom we have already mentioned as being suspicious of the testimony of the senses. In this instance, Descartes also illustrates the values of relaxation in invention, as discussed in the section on Creative Thinking. Descartes was on a mission in Belgium, when illness confined him to his room. He had long been pondering questions of what could be known and how knowledge could be reduced to acceptable units. As Descartes lay on his bed looking out of the window he saw space framed in small squares, as windows were then made. He suddenly found himself imagining the window frame as what today we call a graph with data ploted in two dimensions on horizontal and vertical axes. In this way problems could be broken down into small parts and displayed for inspection. Descartes even originated a formula for clear thinking based on his graph. It was this: (1) Test very carefully everything that goes into the thinking process. (2) Break the problem into small pieces. (3) Arrange the pieces in order—on a graph. (4) Review, and review, and review, and review—till the light comes. Descarte's technique of making a graph has proven of such value that today we see graphs being used wherever statistical information is reported.

There are, naturally, a great many kinds of distribution used to depict the various kinds of information gathered. One very common form, particularly of biological data, is called the normal curve of distribution. It will be found in measuring people for head size or for height or weight; it will be found in measuring the leaves of any tree for length or width; it will be found in comparing race horses for speed. An illustration of the curve and its use is shown below.

A large company, in having a conference for their salesmen, will bring together a thousand men gathered from all parts of the country. Intending to gain some advertising advantage from the convention, the company decides to present each man with a hat, of uniform style, which will be decorated with a bright red band. But the hats must fit or the men will look

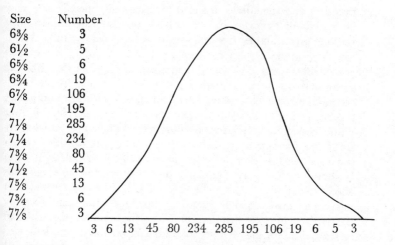

Size	Number
6⅜	3
6½	5
6⅝	6
6¾	19
6⅞	106
7	195
7⅛	285
7¼	234
7⅜	80
7½	45
7⅝	13
7¾	6
7⅞	3

3 6 13 45 80 234 285 195 106 19 6 5 3

Hat sizes Required by One Thousand Soldiers

ridiculous. It would be too cumbersome, however, to write to each man and request him to send his hat size. So the company turns to an army bulletin to find out what sizes of hats would normally be called for by a thousand men. They find the distribution given below, which is a tabulation of the actual hat sizes of a thousand soldiers.

By securing a few extra hats of each size, to meet probable irregularities, the company will be able to provide every salesman with a hat of the proper size.

The statistical worker, even when dealing with biological data, must always remember that the distribution he is working with may not be a normal one, nor even a curve of this type. The normal curve is but one of many different distributions.

Measures of Central Tendency. It is natural for people to seek some easily grasped simple figure to represent a group of data. "I have an eighty-five average," says the student. "My average income for the year was five hundred dollars a month," says the salesman. Such statements of central tendency help a person to grasp the essentials of a question quickly. The method, however, has a number of pitfalls.

There are three common measures of central tendency: the average or *mean,* the median, and the mode. In careless practice, and sometimes in sharp practice, any one of these may be called an average. In a relatively normal distribution, like the one given above, the three measures are nearly alike. When the distribution is perfect they are exactly alike. The mode is the highest point in the distribution, or the class with the greatest frequency; the median is the middle figure in the range counted in from either end; and the mean is the term familiar as the average, that is, all the quantities added and divided by their number. A false conclusion encouraged by the failure to understand an average is that regarding the length of life, which some people believe indicates that nearly everyone will soon be living to be very old. In Roman times this average was about twenty-five years, whereas today it is nearly seventy. It has been getting higher year by year, but until very recently the main cause of this increase was the smaller mortality in infancy. Lately, the diseases of old age are being studied and today there is some greater life expectancy for older people, but not so much as is suggested by the increase of the average length of life from twenty-five to seventy.

Although such misunderstandings from improper application of the measures of central tendency occur everywhere, it is easier to find illustrations in which some special purpose is sought. For instance, a small company has thirty employees and three owner-officers. The salaries of the employees range from five to seven thousand dollars, and the salaries of the officers are twenty-five thousand dollars each. It is not good publicity to report that the average salary of the employees was six thousand dollars and that of the officers was twenty-five thousand. It is better public relations to say that the average salary of all those working for the company approximates seventy-seven hundred dollars. It is always helpful to know what extremes are hidden back of the figures whenever measures of central tendency are used to represent a group. As these extremes can be hidden in different ways by mean, median and mode, the reader should determine which measure is being used, and why.

Measures of Range. Measures of range are very closely related to those of central tendency and often one cannot tell the importance of the central tendency until he knows the range represented. Since body temperature has a very small range of variation its average of 98.6 F. is usually considered representative. If a person's temperature is found to be one degree above the average he is warned that he has a fever. In other circumstances, however, the average does not fit the individual so well, and most people would feel insulted if told that they would be expected to wear an average-sized suit of clothes. In housing, where builders have been impressed by the fact that the average-sized family has three or four children this situation does occur to a greater extent than is desirable. A great preponderance of houses built for sale have been of a size to accomodate such a family, while smaller and larger houses are seldom built.

Range should always be observed as well as central tendency. There are two common measures for this, each having a slightly different use. One is the "standard deviation," which indicates how closely the data surround the average, and the other is the "probable error," which indicates whether the average used is a stable one from an adequate sample, or whether it will be changed significantly when more cases are added.

It is unnecessary to give here the calculation of these measures, which will be found in technical books. In a normal curve of distribution the standard deviation will include the 68 per cent of the cases nearest the average. This deviation is measured along the base line, showing how widely the data scatter. One of the uses of standard deviation is to compare apparently unrelated things. For instance, the standard deviation for body temperature can be compared with the standard deviation for physical size, and this with the standard deviation for the speed of arithmetical calculations, in the same group. It will be found that men vary much more in arithmetical operations than they do in size, and they vary more in size than they do in body temperature. Such information is often useful when examining the interpretation of data.

Whenever averages are quoted, the reader does well to notice whether the range is small, as in body temperature, or large, as in arithmetical calculations, and whether any probable errors are given for the work.

Measures of Relationship-Correlation. Nearly everyone recognizes problems of correlation when they are stated without statistics. At the present time, for instance, there is a big rush among high school graduates to get into "Ivy League" colleges. The assumption is that graduation from an Ivy League college assures one of greater success in life than does graduation from a college less well known. In the same way, some people assume that employment for a few years with General Motors, Ford, or du Pont, will be more likely to make them successful in life than will an equal experience in some small firm. The advertisements tell us every day that all those who eat this or that will be strong and healthy, those that use a certain commodity to smooth down their hair will be popular, and "men of distinction" prefer to drink a certain brand of whiskey.

Statistical techniques are available to determine the correspondence of things said to be related. Does Progressive Education in the grades make a student more or less successful in college? Does belonging to a fraternity result in higher or lower college grades? To what extent is it true that the fashionably dressed young man tends to get ahead in business? When such relationships are claimed one should note first whether they were established intuitively or statistically. If they were intuitively determined one must use his own good sense in examining them. If they were supported with statistics it is necessary to make sure that the statistics used were sound.

Even when correlations have been statistically established, however, they may not indicate cause and effect. Suppose one finds that graduates of Ivy League colleges make more money, on the average, than do graduates of less well-known institutions. No cause for this has been shown. Does this mean that Ivy League colleges give a better education or merely that they are attended by more sons of the rich, and that the wealth of their fathers has been visited, in one way or another, upon their offspring?

A great many things may be correlated without any causal connection. It may be a good year for both cotton crops and peanut crops, but the cotton crop is not the cause of the peanut crop. It may be an unusually good year for oranges in California, when it may be a very bad year for skiing in the mountains nearby; but though the warm weather may be the cause in both cases, bad skiing does not produce good oranges. Sometimes a correlation does not indicate cause and effect and sometimes it does. It is probable that good health helps to produce good spirits, that machinery helps to produce wealth, and that a good education helps to increase one's satisfactions in life. The observer must always determine whether correlation indicates cause and effect before he draws conclusions.

Computers and "Brain Machines." "Brain machines" facilitate many kinds of statistical thinking. Some of them operate with the speed of light permitting calculations to guide gunfire or satellites. They can solve problems that would require years, or even lifetimes, without them. But their use does not contradict logic nor eliminate human thinking. The machines operate on the binary number system and Boole's Algebra of logic. Their use requires special training.

Summary

Probabilities and statistics cover a difficult area where facts, that do not fit into simple homogeneous classes, may be hard to gather. Therefore, a great many errors are made in statistical thinking. Some of these errors are due to lack of information, some to strong motivation that predisposes people to accept favorable results too easily, and some to dishonesty. A number of precautions, such as the following, are advisable to prevent error.

(1) Watch for bias. When management gives data about management, when labor gives out information about labor, or when a manufacturing company publishes information about its new product there is likely to be a distortion of data. A little booklet of selected information for automobile salesmen provides an example. In this booklet a salesman—whether he sells one make or another—can find all the statistics for his car favorably presented.

(2) Observe carefully whether authorities are quoted without their permission with such an introduction as: "In a survey by Harvard University it was found . . . " Read carefully to see whether the conclusion is the same one drawn by Harvard, whether it is applied in some improper context, or whether someone has varied the statistical treatment to support a different conclusion.

(3) When a conclusion is presented, determine how it was reached. Remember, a germ killed in a bottle in someone's scientific laboratory is not quite the same thing as a germ killed in the throat of someone who has a cold.

(4) Note if an adequate sample was used. Toothpastes and patent medicines have been tried out on as few as a dozen people. When samples are too small they are meaningless.

(5) When percentages are given, determine the base from which they are calculated, and sometimes find out the actual quantities they represent.

(6) Make sure that the statistics used are those gathered. For instance, if a group of young men is asked how tall they are they will usually answer with a figure that is, on the average, about an inch taller than their measured height. This exaggeration, which does not happen with girls, is probably an unconscious reaction to the prestige of tall men. In consequence, it would be an error if information of reported height among men was used in a discussion of measured height. It is necessary to watch for these illusive ways of falsifying statistics.

(7) In an examination of statistical conclusions, it is wise to ask whether they are consistent with everything one knows.

Sometimes unusual conclusions are to be reached, but a great deal of statistical error would be exposed if the reader just used his good sense. The conclusions of any apparently unreasonable statistical study should receive a thorough examination.

(8) Further skepticism is necessary when conclusions are projected into the future. A few years ago a well-known statistician, after studying the divorce rate in the United States, predicted that by 1960 there would be as many divorces as marriages. But 1960 has come and gone and the number of divorces still does not approach the number of marriages. It is never possible to tell when some new force will begin to exert its influence. "The Decline and Fall of the West" has not occurred, the World Revolution has not appeared, and even the end of the world, predicted many times, has failed to relieve us of our responsibilities.

We turn away now from the determination of facts and generalizations, to the techniques of reasoning. The next chapter deals with deduction.

Chapter 4

DEDUCTION

DEFINITION OF DEDUCTION

Deduction is reasoning from some generalization to some particular instance consistent with it. An example would be: All spiders spin webs, which is a generalization. The reasoning: This animal is a spider. Therefore this animal will spin a web. Such deductions are common activities of the mind and we have them implied in the proverbs left us by even the most primitive of people. Although not formally stated, the proverb: "Many stones bring down the walnut" suggests what can be done with a particular stone.

A proverb expresses a great deal of experience and usually implies a rule of action that serves to guide a person in particular instances: "Haste makes waste"; "A stitch in time saves nine." Occasionally the statement requires interpretation ("Still waters run deep"), and sometimes it is obvious ("Better lose a jest than a friend"), but in most cases proverbs suggest conformity in situations consistent with them.

It is quite probable that proverbs stimulated the first primitive deductions. It is certain that proverbs bring to mind the two major problems of all generalizations; are they true, and where do they apply.

The determination of the truth of generalizations has already been discussed in the chapter on induction. No one should ever fail to verify the reliability of the facts and generalizations he uses. Problems cannot be solved by reasoning from mistaken facts and generalizations.

The second question, which deals with where generalizations can be applied, is the main problem of deduction. For instance, if it is true that "Virtue is its own reward," does that have any relevance to the problem of how large a donation to make to the Red Cross?

The Greeks were the first people to think scientifically about their generalizations. Successful mathematical deduction may have been the stimulus for this movement. The Greeks had made the extraordinary discovery that the abstract uniformity of time, space, and number systems permitted the determination, by reasoning, of new facts from known facts. Thales of Miletus, early in the sixth century B.C., showed that such propositions as "A circle is bisected by any diameter," need not be established by measurement since it can be proved by reasoning.

By the time of Euclid in 300 B.C. the Greeks knew how to reason by a sequence of deductive steps from a given set of original statements to some particular conclusion.

Aristotle is usually given the credit for formulating the rules of deduction. He demonstrated how one could reason from general truths to specific instances. The classical example is: "All men are mortal. Socrates is a man. Therefore Socrates is mortal." The order here is (1) the statement of a generalization, (2) the identification of an individual instance included in the class described by the generalization, and (3) the application of the generalization to the individual case. It can be simplified still further by saying that one always reasons downward from a generalization describing a class, to the class described, to some individual member of that class.

Deductive logic deals with conclusions that are mandatory if one has accepted certain other beliefs. Facts and generalizations, which must be established by induction, are preliminary to the reasoning. Deduction is applied wholly to reasoning, therefore all deductive errors are errors in reasoning. In the two examples below the deductions are equally sound since they are the same. (1) Since all gold is heavy and this object is gold, it is also heavy. (2) Since all successful men are honest and John is a successful man, John is also honest. The conclusion in the second case may be false because the generalization is not sound, and perhaps John is not so successful as someone has thought. Deduction is merely the means of moving accurately, without observation or measurement, from a given assumption to a conclusion. If the facts or generalizations are in error the conclusion *may* be false. Required further are carefully defined terms and clear concepts.

The means of movement in deduction is the inference which takes leave of a given assumption by means of an act of judgment. For instance, if all canaries are birds, we can also be sure that some birds are canaries. The significance of deduction is that it gives procedures by which an inference can be checked without recourse to "trying it out in practice." To solve problems successfully, of course, one must never forget to apply inductive as well as deductive procedures. All facts and generalizations must be established before it will be useful to reason correctly from them. This requirement being met, a great deal of time and expense can be saved by the application of deductive reasoning.

THE LAWS OF THOUGHT

The so-called laws of thought were devised by Aristotle to make clear the situations in which his principles of deductive reasoning would operate. Today these laws are sometimes criticized. It is said that Aristotle did not himself present them as the laws of thought. If they are laws, continue the critics, they are not inclusive. Finally, they are unnecessary, it is said, or have been better stated in other places. These criticisms are answered by the assertion that although Aristotle did not specifically codify his requirements as laws he did state them as principles necessary to deductive thinking. It is also contended that with the connotations of words as well as their denotations to deal with the recognition of these "laws" is very useful. Finally, for those who are not advanced thinkers or experts in logic the statement of Aristotle's laws is helpful. In consequence the three laws are given here: (1) the law of identity, (2) the law of contradiction, and (3) the law of the excluded middle.

The Law of Identity. The law of identity states that a term must have the same meaning throughout an argument. It is the law of identity that led Descartes to protest that information acquired through the senses is too unreliable to be accepted as true. The reader will recall the illustration from Chapter II in which hard wax, soft wax, and liquid wax were all designated as "wax." That particular difficulty was removed by giving the temperature of the wax in each case, but the problem remains. An argument about democracy would be futile if the term meant to one person what it means to the average American and meant to his opponent what it means to the average Communist.

The Law of Contradiction. This law states that one cannot assert and deny the same thing of the same concept or class; for instance, about a man who in general is very wise but foolish about money. Aristotelian logic would not permit him to be classified, at one time, as both wise and foolish, and still that is what he seems to be. Teen-agers sometimes complain that they are termed both adults and children at the same time— adults if there is work to do and children if they wish to govern themselves.

The Law of the Excluded Middle. The law of the excluded middle states that A is either B or not B. For example, in a presidential campaign in the United States a candidate finds either that he has been elected president or he has not been elected president. Again, when one takes an examination and either passes it or fails, when he applies to be licensed as a doctor or lawyer and either obtains his license or does not obtain it, the law of excluded middle is illustrated. In these cases there is no middle ground. A person is either included in a class or excluded from it. Such situations are found everywhere. Carbon is either an element or it is not an element. A whale is either a mammal or it is not a mammal. Tokyo is either a Japanese city or it is not a Japanese city. The earth is a planet or it is not a planet.

But there are other situations in which there is no sharp dividing line between concepts. Day eases off into twilight before night comes, and there is a period when it seems to be neither day nor night. Dividing lines between the sane and the insane, the young and the old, the wise and the foolish are lacking. It is impossible to exclude the middle ground between these pairs of concepts, and consequently they will create difficulties if used in deductive procedures.

An example is found in trials where temporary insanity is claimed by the defendant. The law, in the past, has treated men as either sane or insane. But actually, sanity is a matter of one's responsibility, which is not an either-or quality but a relative one. In murder trials, when the plea of insanity is made, it has often proved almost impossible to determine the defendant's classification in accordance with the law's either-or definition.

Modern statistics, by dividing data into the discrete and the continuous has found legitimate ways to handle the latter type. The continuous data occupy intervals in a distribution which are different from simple classes and are treated in different ways.

It should perhaps be noted here that there have been some criticisms of the whole basis of Aristotelian thinking. The complaints usually follow this mode: Linneaus is said to have advanced biology tremendously with his development of the art of classification, but then his system fossilized and has clung like a dead weight to modern biology, holding it back. Sir Isaac Newton enabled physics to become a science, but then dominated the field so completely that for years he inhibited its further development. In the same way, it is claimed, Aristotle brought organization out of the confusion of primitive thinking, but his authority finally became so great that the world of thought crystalized in Aristotelian forms with a consequent detriment to modern thinking.

These criticisms deal with the problem of change. The most noteworthy of the complainants are the Hegelians, the Existentialists, and the Semanticists. Let us examine them briefly.

Hegel believed that the universe is changing continually in the direction of completion and perfection. He felt that traditional logic did not provide for the gradual continuity of this change. For him, A is never completely A because it is always becoming B. His solution was described in three steps: "Thesis, antithesis, synthesis." In the first step the thinker accepts the object of his thought as a unit. In the second step antithesis, or opposition, is introduced as the stage of skeptical analysis, reducing the previous unity to multiple differences and contradictory parts. The third step builds from the parts some new unity with a higher organization. The continual change goes on primarily in the direction of opposition; thesis always conflicts with antithesis to reach a new synthesis. The Hegelian sees the world filled with triads, processing the never-ending change.

Hegelian logic has had considerable influence but can be

criticized as proceding from theory to fact. It is by no means certain that the universe is being completed and perfected by means of the conflict, reduction and synthesis of opposites. Hegelian thinking tends to force facts into the mold of theory as the Communists do in molding facts to support Marx and Lenin. As emphasizing the necessity of adjusting thought to the changes taking place in the world, however, Hegel's influence has undoubtedly been beneficial.

The Existentialists are a group of people identified by an attitude rather than by a method of thinking. Disillusioned, perhaps, by the great wars, they have concluded that the critical problem for each man is his own individual existence, and that his problem is one of choice and decision as much as it is of reason. Existentialists are wary of any kind of systematic thinking. Each man's problem is too immediate to be subordinated to general principles. Every person is as unique as his finger prints, and a man's own life is his total wealth. The Existentialist ends his thinking in anguish, and sometimes in despair when he considers the terrible responsibility that he cannot avoid of making the decisions and choices that are to determine his own destiny in this labyrinth of eternity. No new methods of thought, however, have been presented by the Existentialists.

The Semanticists, for the most part, have been writers and other persons interested in the art of communication. Their complaint is that many words retain old meanings even when they are applied to new situations. This happens. Words such as temperament, personality and democracy must be continually re-defined or they misrepresent the facts and experiences to which they refer. But even though the demand for repeated re-definition of terms is justified it does not call for a revolt against our whole system of thinking. The Semanticists could not do without such concepts as the number seven which is not becoming number etight or changing into something else. Both stability and adjustment to change are needed for sound thinking and both are provided for by the so called "Aristotelian thinking."

To reiterate: Our thinking is based on percepts, which are subject to continual change. Just as Heraclitus could not step into the same river twice, a person never repeats two identical perceptions. These perceptions, formed into groups, produce concepts which, synthesized from many percepts, change less than do the original percepts. Finally, concepts grouped and described produce laws and principles which change less than the concepts. Repeated examination of these elements is needed for valid thinking.

PROPOSITIONS

A proposition, which is a sentence that expresses a judgment, is the unit of reasoning. Several characteristics identify a proposition. It must be either true or false. It is the judgment, not of a fact, but of a relationship. To say "The sun is cold," is just as good a proposition as the statement, "The sun is hot." Whenever we doubt something, believe it, or know it, and state this judgment we have presented a proposition. Possible judgments are found all around us in relating the percepts and concepts that we have formed: the sun is hot, the water is wet, the sky is blue. We go to form more complex judgments: the sun makes the water warm. Finally, we have an organized system of concepts related by many interlocking judgments: pens and pencils will do the same work as type-writers, but more slowly; writing done with a pencil is not as neat nor as lasting as that done with a pen; handwriting is more difficult to read than typewriting. A proposition is a statement, such as those given above, in which a judgment is made of the relationship existing among the named percepts and concepts.

The nature of judgment is not improved by eloquence, nor are propositions dependant upon the language that carries them. A proposition can be translated from one language to another without loss. "Las Puertas son cerradas a llavo" (*in Spanish*) is just as good a proposition as "The doors are locked." It is the meaning or judgment that is the essence of the proposition.

A proposition is always a sentence, but not all sentences are propositions. The following expressions are not propositions: "How would you like to own a circus?" "Please go!" "What time is it?"

Kinds of Propositions. There are five kinds of propositions; categorical, hypothetical, alternative, disjunctive, and conjunctive.

Categorical. The categorical proposition states a judgment simply and directly, as for example, "Poverty is no sin." It is the fundamental form of judgment, and it will here be given the most attention. This proposition has a subject term about which something is asserted or denied; a connective term, or *copula,* which is some form of the verb to be, and a predicate term indicating that which is asserted about the subject. In common usage, the copula is sometimes merely implied and can easily be added without changing the meaning of the statement. "All men die" stated in good propositional form would be, "All men are animals that die." "Haste makes waste" becomes, "Haste is an activity that makes waste."

There are several forms of categorical propositions.

(1) Some propositions state predication, as "Man is an intelligent animal." Properties or qualities are attributed here to a concept or class of concepts.

(2) The second categorical proposition is one of class inclusion, in which a concept or class of concepts is said to belong to a more inclusive class. "All men are vertebrates" is an example of this, since vertebrates compose a far more numerous class than men.

(3) In class-membership propositions we find an individual placed in a class. "Frank is a lawyer"; "George is a Canadian." One must be careful not to attempt to classify two or more individuals at one time. It would be incorrect to consider "Frank and I are lawyers" or "all three of us are lawyers" as properly stated class-membership propositions. One could say, "Frank and I are members of a group all of whom are lawyers." In this case the proposition becomes one of class inclusion, as in (2) above.

(4) In other propositions the subject is said to be identical with the predicate, as in: "A cube is a regular solid of six equal square sides." The proposition may be read either way: "A regular solid of six equal square sides is a cube."

(5) The general proposition is a modern form not used by the Greeks, who thought that all classes, as in the statement "All vertebrates are animals," would be represented by specific instances. In modern logic the propositional function has been invented. This is a judgment which leaves the membership

in a proposition unspecified, although it is represented by **X**. Propositions of this kind are very useful in symbolic logic where they save work in stating such cases as: "Of the men in this group, one (not yet identified) is the murderer of John Doe.

Hypothetical. The hypothetical proposition expresses an if-then relationship about an undetermined fact: If it is a gas it is a form of matter." Hypothetical propositions are often used by scientists who must examine situations before all the facts are known, and by others who have the problem of predicting the consequences if certain things should happen. Scientists frequently search for pertinent facts by creating a hypothesis as a guide. For instance, a geologist might assume that "If there is a gas inside the earth it will probably tend to expand and escape," and then search for escaping gas.

Alternative. The alternative proposition presents two possibilities: "There was never a promise made but that it was either broken or kept." In this case, the alternatives are mutually exclusive and only one of them can be true. But it is not always so; in the statement, "He is either crazy or badly mistaken, " both alternatives could be true. The subject matter of alternative propositions must be carefully examined to determine whether the alternatives are mutually exclusive.

Disjunctive. The disjunctive proposition specifically states that one of the two alternative judgments must be false: "A man cannot be both healthy and sick at the same time."

Conjunctive. The conjunctive propositions simply joins two categorical propositions; both of them may be true, or both may be false, or one may be true and the other false: "In hard times the wise man cuts his expenses and the foolish man cuts his throat."

ANALYSIS OF THE CATEGORICAL PROPOSITION

The categorical proposition, as we have seen, contains a subject and predicate, each relating to a concept or class of concepts. These two terms, since they may be related positively or negatively, and since they designate either a whole class or a restricted part of it, permit one to make four kinds of judgments, which are identified by the letters, A,E,I, and O, as follows.

A. All scientific knowledge is profitable.

E. No scientific knowledge is profitable.

I. Some scientific knowledge is profitable.

O. Some scientific knowledge is not profitable.

The A and E propositions are said to be *universal* or *distributed,* since their subjects refer to a whole class of "all" scientific knowledge. The I and O propositions are said to be *particular* or *undistributed,* since they refer to only a part of the groups about which they make a statement, as "some" scientific knowledge. Propositions A an I are positive, and E and O are negative.

Propositions about an individual, such as, "Abraham Lincoln was a great president"; and "Plato's Republic is not a novel," may be construed as universal propositions. They make statements about an individual as an individual, not as a member of a class.

The distribution of terms we have discussed so far relates only to the subject of the propositions. The predicates, however, can also be distributed. This is usually not stated explicitly but is determined by the kind of a proposition, even though the distribution of the predicate does not always agree with the distribution of the subject. In proposition A, "All scientific knowledge is profitable," the term, scientific knowledge, is obviously distributed since *all* scientific knowledge is specified. But since there is no reference in the predicate to all profitable things, the predicate is undistributed. In the E proposition both the subject and the predicate are distributed. In the proposition "No scientific knowledge is profitable," all scientific knowledge and all profitable things are included in the statement. Particular attention must be given in E propositions to the subject, because of an assumption of meaning that is sometimes called the "atmosphere" effect. If the E proposition "All dishonesty is not profitable," is stated, a person is likely to assume from general language usage that "If all dishonesty is not profitable," then some is. But this is not intended. The implication of the E proposition is that *no* dishonesty is profitable. It is usually wise to state an E proposition unambiguosly to avoid this error.

In negative propositions, both E and O, the predicate is distributed automatically, since the denial of an attribute implies complete denial. The E proposition asserts something about all profitable things, namely, that none of them is dishonesty. The O proposition, "Some dishonesty is not profitable," implies that if all profitable thigns were grouped together, no dishonesty would be included.

Negative propositions distribute their predicates automatically. This is not true of positive propositions. For instance, "All Socialists are supporters of Social Security" does not tell us anything about all supporters of Social Security. It would be fallacious to conclude that "All supporters of Social Security are socialists." The statement "some study is profitable" does not imply that some study is not profitable. Perhaps, but not necessarily, all study is profitable.

One must learn to read every negative proposition carefully to make sure that it is really negative, that is, that some attribute is denied to the subject. A negative can be used descriptively in an affirmative proposition. "No matter how shoddy the goods, you can always find a customer" is a positive statement, but "No merchant has the right to mislead his customers" is negative. Many mistakes are made in thinking because people are not accustomed to scrutinizing negatives and sometimes use them carelessly, as in the following excerpt from a student's letter: "Dear Mom: The doctor reports that it is not true that I cannot read without harm to my eyes." (See clarification, page 78)

Summarizing the distribution of terms, we find that the only terms that are always distributed are the subjects of the universal propositions, A and E, and the predicates of the negative propositions, E and O. The predicates of A propositions may be distributed in the case of propositions of identity, as "Dr. Robert Goddard is the man who shot the first rocket powered with liquid fuel." Another case is that "All pure gold, and only pure gold, has an atomic weight of 197.2."

Visual Aids. Leonard Euler, a Swiss mathematician and scientist, popularized a method of visualizing relationships given in propositions. He represented the terms of a proposition by circles and, by arranging the circles, indicated inclusion or exclusion of the terms.

We have then:

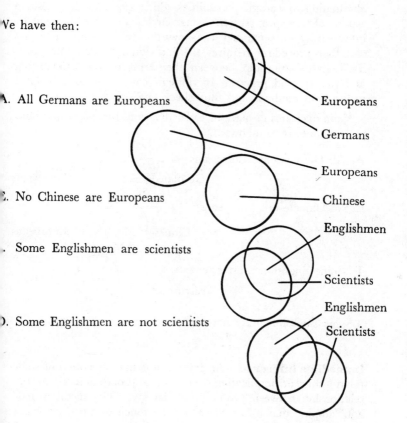

A. All Germans are Europeans — Europeans / Germans

B. No Chinese are Europeans — Europeans / Chinese

C. Some Englishmen are scientists — Englishmen / Scientists

D. Some Englishmen are not scientists — Englishmen / Scientists

John Venn, an English logician whom we have already noted as one of the originators of frequency probability, worked out a variation of the Euler circles in 1894, about a hundred years after their first appearance. This system uses overlapping circles, no matter what the propositions are. Venn shades out areas where the population is zero, draws a line through an area in which there are some members, and leaves blank areas for which no specifications are given. He examines a proposition in terms of its negatives, using lines and shading to indicate the elimination of certain possibilities. Euler examines the positive aspect of the proposition, using circles that are concentric, intersecting, or separated to show the relationship. The use of either procedure requires the individual to determine precisely the relationship between the terms of the proposition, and this is good practice. In difficult cases it is often helpful to use both methods and thus check one's work.

Venn diagrams in place of Euler diagrams for the propositions given above are as follows:

A. All Germans are Europeans

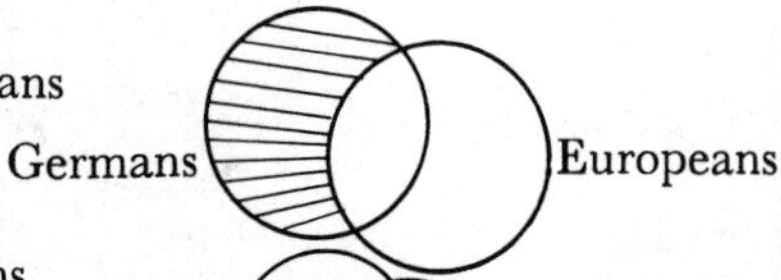

Germans   Europeans

E. No Chinese are Europeans

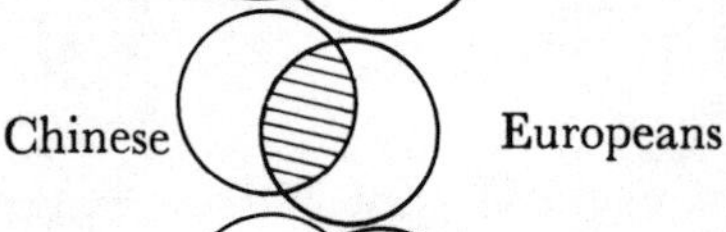

Chinese   Europeans

I. Some Englishmen are scientists

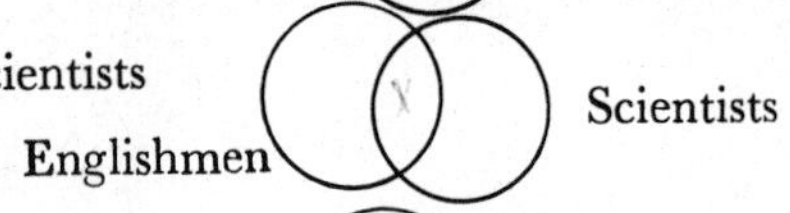

Englishmen   Scientists

O. Some Englishmen are not scientists

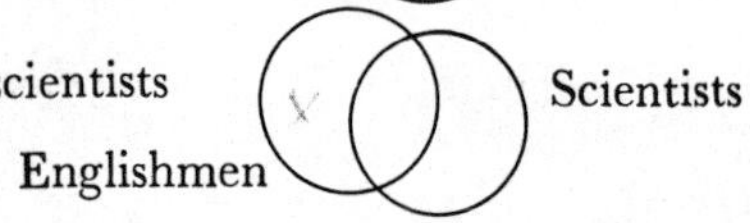

Englishmen   Scientists

Immediate Inference. An inference is the perception of some relationship or implication found in a proposition or in the relationship between propositions. To say, "The metal is red-hot," implies that it had better not be touched, but discovering that implication and stating it is an inference. Statements of this kind, "if hot, don't touch," are often called "if-then" relationships and are the basis of deductive thinking.

When a number of conclusions are inferred from one proposition, the procedure is called Immediate Inference. "A black hen may lay white eggs" implies the possibility that a black hen may not lay black eggs.

If we state A,E,I, and O propositions using the same terms, we find certain fixed relationships among them. This type of

Immediate Inference is called Opposition. A visual aid called the Square of Opposition has long been in use to make clear these relationships.

Square of Opposition. The statement "Large families bring poverty," put into the four forms called for by the Square of Opposition, gives the following results:

A. All large families bring poverty

E. No large families bring poverty

I. Some large families bring poverty

O. Some large families do not bring poverty

The Square of Opposition

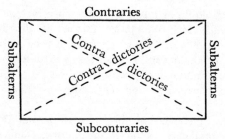

In comparing the universal propositions A and E, we can see that both cannot be true, although both can be false. It is impossible that at the same time all large families are, and are not, the cause of poverty, but it is possible that both statements are false and that some large families bring poverty and some do not.

Many fallacious arguments are based on the assumption that if one has proved one universal proposition to be wrong, its contrary is therefore right. When it has been demonstrated that (A) "All Republicans are isolationists" is false, it cannot be assumed that (E) "No Republicans are isolationists" is true. This type of argument can be made, however, if one goes diagonally across the Square of Opposition from A to O. If it is false that "All Republicans are isolationists" (A), it must be true that "Some Republicans are not isolationists" (O), for these are contradictories, and if one is false the other must be true.

Universals contain the particulars subsumed under them, so that if the universal is true the particular must also be true. If all vertebrates are animals, then some are; if no vertebrates are animals, then some are not. But the reverse is not true, and one cannot assume the universal from the particular and conclude that because some animals are not vertebrates none are. This assumption of the universal from the particular is one of the commonest fallacies in everyday arguments. The fact that some teen-agers make trouble for their parents does not mean that all do.

Making distinctions between simple A, E, I and O propositions helps one to understand the same distinctions between complex ones. For debaters and contract-writers the practice of making such distinctions can be very useful.

Further techniques of immediate inference include conversion and obversion, which emphasize factors of distribution and which clarify negatives. These techniques can be used separately or combined, producing still further forms such as contraposition and inversion. Analysis will be limited here to the two fundamental forms, conversions and obversion.

Conversion. In conversion the original proposition is turned around; the predicate becomes the subject, and the subject becomes the predicate. The quality, that is, the characteristic of being positive or negative, remains the same, and the meaning maintains its consistency. If the original is true, the converse is true. "All chemistry is useful knowledge" converts to "Some useful knowledge is chemistry." Two rules control conversion: (1) the positive or negative quality of the proposition must remain the same, and (2) no term can be distributed in the converse that was not distributed in the original. In the statement above, the distributed term "all useful knowledge" is not implied in the original and so cannot be contained in the converse.

Since E propositions always have distributed predicates, they convert without limitation. "The duckbill of Australia is not a bird" becomes "Among birds one will never find the Australian duckbill."

When one attempts to convert an O proposition, he is prohibited from doing so by the rule that no term may be distributed in the converse that was not distributed in the original. "Some men are not wealthy" cannot be converted to "Some wealthy individuals are not men," because in the latter case the negative distributes the word "men" and means not to be found anywhere among all men, whereas the original statement was about "some men."

Obversion. Obversion is a technique by which a positive proposition becomes negative, and a negative one positive. A,E,I, and O propositions can all be validly obverted, although it must be done carefully to avoid errors. The obversion of a universal proposition remains universal, A being changed to E, and E to A. The obversion of a particular proposition remains particular, I being changed to O, or O to I. The underlying principle of obversion is that two negatives make an affirmative. "All gas is composed of molecules" becomes "Gas is composed of nothing that is not molecular."

The procedure of obversion allows the subject to retain its original form as it proceeds by negating the copula and the predicate. Thus, the quality of the proposition is changed but only the predicate and the copula are involved in the obversion. "Weather predictions based on weather signs are not likely to be accurate" becomes "Weather predictions based on weather signs are likely to be inaccurate." A common error that creeps into obversion is the one of changing the predicate into a form that is not the exact contrary of the original form. For instance, if one obverts "Most boys like vacation" to "Most boys do not like to go to school," he will be committing this error, since "going to school" is not the exact opposite of "vacation."

Obversion can be used to clarify a negative or to make a positive statement more emphatic by changing it into a double negative.

Original: Officeholders must not be nonresidents.
Obverse: Officeholders must be residents.
Original: A good soldier obeys an order.
Obverse: A good soldier does not disobey an order.
Original: The song is good.
Obverse: The song is not bad.

The difficult statement given earlier, "Dear Mom: The doctor reports that it is not true that I cannot read without harm to my eyes," can now be simplified. There are three negatives here. If we obvert the main clause we get, "The doctor says it is true that I can read without harm to my eyes."

THE CATEGORICAL SYLLOGISM

The if-then relationship is the basis of deductive reasoning. In our study of immediate inference we examined the implications of a single proposition. Deductive logic, however, goes farther than this, following the implications of a generalization to specific instances subsumed under it.

When one seeks to apply a generalization, however, one meets a difficulty. "Men are thinking beings" is a generalization. How does one get from the generalization to a spot where its implications are helpful?

If one analyzes a categorical generalization, one finds it a statement about two classes or groups of things. In "All men are thinking beings," the groups are (1) all men and (2) thinking beings. These statements are interesting as far as they go, but before we can apply them to specific instances, we must have some indication of class membership. Man is a thinking being. John Jones is a man. Therefore we can make the statement, "John Jones is a thinking being." The statement of class membership is the means of stepping from the generalization to the particular instance. Such a combination of propositions— one generalization about a class or group, one giving an instance of class or group membership, and one a deduced conclusion regarding the class member—is called a *categorical syllogism*. As far as is known this form of reasoning was originated by Aristotle.

Rules of the Syllogism. In the example just cited the syllogism was found to consist of three propositions, and this requirement can be given as the first rule of the syllogism. It is impossible to proceed from a generalization to an application in only two steps. "Difficulties reveal a man's character. This is a difficulty" leaves our thought unfinished. "Difficulties reveal a man's character. This situation reveals a man's character" is disconnected and unverified. "Difficulties reveal a man's character. This is a difficulty. Therefore this situation will reveal a man's character" is valid. If an attempt is made to use four propositions on the same task, the result will be ambiguous and frustrating.

Difficulties reveal the characters of men.

This is a difficulty.

Napoleon overcame many difficulties.

Napoleon could have overcome this difficulty.

The last proposition is not proved. Four propositions bring in attached but unfinished ideas which are too many for logical reasoning. A syllogism consists of three and only three propositions.

At this point, it will be well to return to the Euler and Venn diagrams, so that they can be used in examining the syllogisms that appear in the following pages. These diagrams have been demonstrated in propositions with two terms. To use them with syllogisms having three terms we must use three circles, each circle representing a term. In the diagram below will be found the Euler and Venn visualization of the following syllogism:

Quartz is a mineral

This object is quartz

Therefore, this object is a mineral.

Euler:

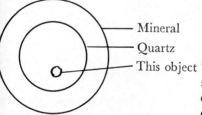

Mineral
Quartz
This object

Quartz is a mineral and so the quartz-circle is placed within the mineral circle. "This object" is quartz and so is represented by a small circle inside the quartz circle.

Venn:

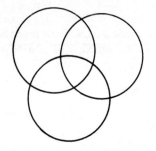

Always draw the empty Venn circles overlapping in this way before examining the syllogism that is to be diagrammed.

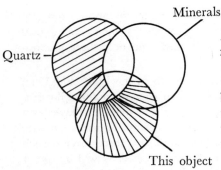

Minerals

Quartz —

This object

After reading the syllogism, name one circle after each term, and shade out the population that is said to be zero. Put one line through the areas where the population is "some." Leave the unspecified areas blank.

In the categorical syllogism there are three and only three separate terms, each one of which is used twice. These three are called the major, middle, and minor term. The student must learn to identify these terms in order to analyze a syllogism properly. The middle term is never found in the conclusion but is found in both premises, which are the two propositions that state the generalization, identify a member of the class specified, and thus lead to the conclusion.

In this syllogism: All insects are invertebrates

The ant is an insect

The ant is an invertebrate

Insect is found in both premises and is absent from the conclusion; it must, therefore, be the middle term. If this syllogism is to be valid, this term must be distributed in one of the premises, as it is in "all insects." Since the middle term represents a class about which a judgment is made, all the class must be specified; otherwise a conclusion might be accepted that was true of some only, and not true of the particular instance specified.

A fallacy even more common than failing to distribute the middle term is that of using a middle term ambiguously as in the following illustration:

All Americans speak English

All Brazilians are Americans

All Brazilians speak English

The term Americans is used in two different senses, and so is the equivalent of two terms, making four for the syllogism. *Americans,* in the first premise, refers to residents of the United States. In the second premise, *Americans* refers to residents of the two American continents.

The major term can always be recognized as the predicate of the conclusion. It is also the subject of the major premise which is the proposition that carries the generalizing statement with which the argument begins (it need not be written first).

The minor term in a syllogism is the term, usually a specific one, that occurs as the subject of the conclusion. The premise in which it occurs is the minor premise:

All hailstones are frozen raindrops

This object is a hailstone

This object is a frozen raindrop

This object is the specific instance about which a conclusion is drawn. It is the minor term of the syllogism. *Raindrops* are the predicate of the conclusion. This identifies the term as the major term and the premise in which it occurs. "All hailstones are frozen raindrops" is the major premise.

One must start with correct major and minor premises if one is to reach a sound conclusion. The correctness of these premises is a matter for induction to determine, as we have already seen.

Individual premises are said to be *true* or *false*. Deduction, which we are examining here, concentrates on the forms of reasoning and such reasoning is said to be *valid* if it is correct and *invalid* if it is incorrect. It is possible to reason validly with mistaken generalizations or undetermined facts, although correct reasoning from mistaken premises leads to mistaken conclusions. Sound thinking requires facts that are true and reasoning that is sound.

Seven rules guide the use of the syllogism: (1) There must be three, and only three propositions; and there must be three and only three terms, and these terms must be used in the same sense throughout.

(2) The middle term must be distributed at least once in the premises.

(3) A term must not be distributed in the conclusion if it was not distributed in at least one of the premises. It is not valid to conclude something about all the members of a group when information has been given about some only.

An injury is a painful thing

All injuries are time consuming

Therefore all painful things are time consuming.

In this syllogism information has been given about only "a painful thing." Therefore, no conclusion about "all painful things" can be drawn. This error, incidentally, is a very common one. If the average man would be constantly alert to the distinction between *all* and *some* he would save himself from many a mistake.

(4) No conclusion can be drawn from two undistributed premises. If one recalls that the purpose of a syllogism is to deduce that something true of a class is true of a smaller class or of an individual, one can see that this is impossible unless the whole class is represented in the argument. Observe this attempt: Some men (of undetermined hair color) are Frenchmen

Some Frenchmen are blackhaired

Therefore, some men (of undetermined hair color) are blackhaired.

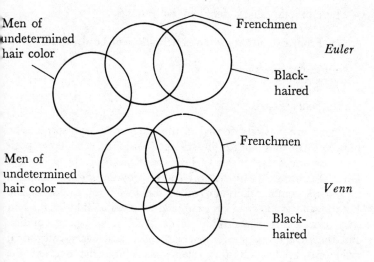

Men of undetermined hair color

Frenchmen

Euler

Black-haired

Men of undetermined hair color

Frenchmen

Venn

Black-haired

In the Venn diagram the overlapping areas of "men of undetermined hair color" and "blackhaired men" may or may not have members. To be valid a conclusion must be proved beyond question (people are sometimes disturbed when they see a conclusion that appears to be correct, but find that the reasoning is invalid. Many conclusions, however, are correct but unproven).

(5) If one of the premises is undistributed, the conclusion must be undistributed.

Some winds are violent

All violence is dangerous

Therefore some winds are dangerous

There is no possibility of getting a distributed, or universal, conclusion from the above syllogism.

(6) If there is one negative premise, the conclusion must be negative.

No fish has lungs
The shark is a fish
Therefore the shark does not have lungs

(7) From two negatives no conclusion can be drawn.

No fish has lungs
The whale is not a fish
(No conclusion is possible)

There are various forms of the categorical syllogism. The middle term may appear in different positions, and these positions determine what are called the *figures* of the syllogism. Different combinations of A,E,I and O propositions may be used, and these combinations are called the *moods* of the syllogism. Figures and moods can be examined at considerable length and may form a sort of shorthand to determining syllogistic validity. But the rules given above cover all cases, and every categorical syllogism can be solved by their means and the help of the Euler and Venn diagrams. So, figures and moods will be left to those interested enough to look them up in more extended treatments.

CONDITIONAL THINKING

Conditional, or hypothetical, thinking usually takes the form of two clauses introduced by "if" and "then". In such thinking a conclusion is drawn from a hypothetical statement. If this kind of thinking is to be done correctly, certain conditions of validity must be met; otherwise the conclusions drawn will probably be invalid. It is necessary here to make a distinction between antecedent and consequent. In the proposition "If it is a gas, it is a form of matter," the position of the terms as antecedent and consequent cannot be reversed. Should we say, "If it is a matter, it is a form of gas," this converse of the original statement would be invalid. This principle becomes obvious in the statement of other hypothetical propositions. "If the grade is steep the car will stall" does not justify the statement that "If the car stalls the grade is steep." Nor does the hypothetical proposition "If you want a thing well done, do it yourself" guarantee that "If you do a thing yourself it will be well done."

When a hypothetical proposition is used in a syllogism, it always becomes the major premise, and the minor premise remains categorical. The antecedent can be affirmed or the consequent denied, and a valid conclusion can be drawn in either case. Other possibilities are invalid, as we can see.

1. *Valid*. The antecedent is affirmed.

> If water is pure it is tasteless
> This water is pure
> Therefore it is tasteless

2. *Invalid*. The antecedent is denied.

> If water is pure it is tasteless
> This water is not pure
> Therefore it is not tasteless

3. *Invalid*. The consequent is affirmed.

> If water is pure it is tasteless
> This water is tasteless
> Therefore it is pure

4. *Valid*. The consequent is denied.

> If water is pure it is tasteless
> This water is not tasteless
> Therefore it is not pure

The reader can check the validity of any of the statements above by rewriting them as categorical syllogisms. Also he may use the Euler or Venn diagrams. Remember that valid means proved. A conclusion that is possible but not certain, is invalid.

Number 3, above, with affirmed consequent becomes:

All pure water is tasteless

This drink is tasteless

Therefore this drink is pure water

The syllogism is invalid because the middle term is not distributed.

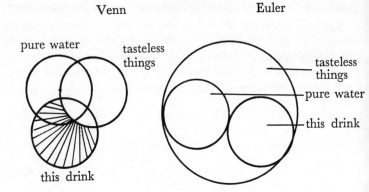

One rule governs the hypothetical syllogism. The minor premise must either affirm the antecedent or deny the consequent. One of the commonest errors is to affirm the consequent: "If this were a diamond it would scratch marble. It does scratch marble. Therefore it is a diamond.

Conditional thinking is useful in the search for facts as when an automobile refuses to run and the trouble might be in the gas line, the carburetor, or the electrical system. Even though one does not realize it, he often begins his search with a hypothetical proposition: "If it is the electrical system, the lights will not go on."

There are other forms of conditional thinking besides the hypothetical, such as the alternative, the disjunctive, and the dilemma, but they are not so fundamental and we shall leave them to books concerned exclusively with deductive logic. In general, conditional thinking points out a lack of knowledge which would permit one to proceed with categorical propositions and syllogisms. "If this animal is an addax, it would have spiral, twisted horns." "If these fingerprints belong to Mr. X, he must have been in the room where the murder was committed."

SUMMARY

The categorical syllogism is the best instrument for testing inferences from established knowledge, and inductive processes are the best means of determining facts. Having examined both of these processes, we are now familiar with all the techniques needed to solve any problem. It is as though we had built a house and were ready to live in it. In solving problems the inductions must be sound; that is, the facts and generalizations must be true, and the reasoning must be valid.

Chapter 5

THINKING APPLIED TO EVERYDAY PROBLEMS

Inductive and deductive methods provide the techniques for solving problems; induction verifies facts and establishes generalizations, while deduction assures the validity of the reasoning. But while induction and deduction are disciplined, well-recognized procedures, the problems to be solved are as devious as a man's fingerprints. It would seem at first that nothing can be done with problems except to meet them individually, but on closer examination it appears that, even as fingerprints, they can be classified. Most of the problems that men meet fit roughly into one or another of the following five classes: (1) Problems of creative thinking; (2) problems of definition; (3) problems of choice, or decision; (4) problems of procedure where the question is "how to do it"; and (5) problems of explanation. The examination of these five classes of problems will help one meet his own specific difficulties.

PROBLEMS OF CREATIVE THINKING

Creativeness Defined as the Eduction of Correlates. We may define creativeness as the discovery of new and meaningful relationships between ideas or things. In a changing world the old ways of doing things are frequently found wanting. Every change in the environment calls for some new response to meet it. Automation brings an endless stream of new problems to management; the evolution of backward people brings new problems to government; and modern methods of transportation, manufacturing, and marketing have required everyone to be creative or be left behind.

Grasping new relationships often comes so spontaneously, suddenly, and frequently to some people, and so seldom to others that the process seems at first to be incomprehensible. But it has yielded to analysis and is named the *Eduction of Correlates*. This is a rather formidable name for a simple process. *Eduction* means "bringing out" *Correlates* are things that are logically related. Suppose one is asked to educe correlates, that is to think of associations, for *white*. One may educe *snow, milk, egg, ivory, alabaster*—things that are white. Or he may think of *black,* the opposite of white. There is no definite end to this procedure, and so one may go on to white man, white duck, white stone, and white cloud—until he runs out of ideas.

The eduction of correlates is not always creative. When one merely brings forth things from his memory that have been stored there and places them in the same order in which he learned them or has often seen them, there is nothing new or creative in the process. But when he puts the ideas brought forth in new and unusual relationships, as pieces are placed in playing a chess game, he may produce something new that is worth retaining. In this way it is possible to work at creative thinking.

Let us illustrate with some unconventional eductions. Given the basic idea of a cow, the eduction "cows give milk" could not be called creative. Neither could the eduction "cow's milk is good for you." Some years ago, however, some one educed the idea of *contented* cows giving good milk, and this slightly unfamiliar idea provided the cue for a very successful advertising slogan. Also, some years ago, Gelett Burgess educed the idea of a purple cow and worked it into a little verse that became quite famous.

> I never saw a purple cow,
>
> I never hope to see one;
>
> But I can tell you, anyhow,
>
> I'd rather see than be one.

Here we have the novel associations of cow and purple and also of a person being a cow. It is probable that Gelett Burgess had to arrange and rearrange these eductions in a number of ways before he was satisfied with the result. Though "The Purple Cow" is hardly great poetry, it serves as a good example of creative thinking.

Writers, artists, scientists, philosophers, inventors—people who think creatively in any field—all educe correlates as the essential process of their creativity. The question is how they go about finding the correlate that, once found, is seen to be so very fitting.

Aristotle, in formulating deductive logic, laid the groundwork for educing correlates. Each individual object had a corresponding form that belonged to some category. The classification was determined by judgments that might prove to be either true or false. These judgments appear in propositions in which something is affirmed or denied. Aristotle found ten possible categories of affirmation or denial.

(1) Substance, as in "This is made of aluminum."

(2) Quality, as in "This diamond is blue-white."

(3) Quantity, as in "There are four beavers."

(4) Relation, as in "Gold is heavier than silver."

(5) Place, as in "It happened in London."

(6) Time, as in "He was born in 1900."

(7) Condition, as in "John is sitting down."

(8) Relatively permanent condition or state, as in "Helen is a mother."

(9) Activity, as in "Fred is swimming."

(10) Passivity, as in "Joe is having his hair cut."

All judgments, thought Aristotle, fall into one of these ten categories. This suggests the possibility, though Aristotle did not mention it, of taking a problem and testing it in all of these ten categories of judgment.

Immanuel Kant suggested a different set of categories. Kant believed that the concepts which men have concerning nature, as described by the various sciences, are determined partly *a priori* (before experience) by the nature of the mind. In brief, the mind has some resemblance to a locomotive that must run on rails because that is its nature, and these required ways are Kant's categories: (1) quantity; (2) quality; (3) relation; and (4) modality (possibility, probability, necessity). One cannot think of anything, says Kant, without thinking of it as having a certain quantity, quality, relation to other things, and modality.

Hegel, following a short time after Kant, in Germany, developed a system based on what he considered the nature of the evolving world. Continual change and development is brought about throughout nature, Hegel believed, through the conflict of opposites. His formula is usually given in the terms of thesis, antithesis, synthesis. It may be assumed that any phenomenon will conflict with its opposite reaching finally a synthesis of opposing forces. This synthesis then conflicts with its opposite, reaching another synthesis. Thus, the world continually changes as it slowly works its way toward perfection.

In using this system for creative thinking, one starts from any point, or problem, educes its opposite, and examines the situation for a possible synthesis.

It has recently been suggested that beside the formal categories of Aristotle and Kant, and the dialectic of Hegel, emotional or functional categories can be used. The functional categories associate, for instance, everything that cuts: knives, mowing machines, scissors, razors, saws and the like. Emotional categories relate things of the same emotional tone, as solutions to problems that are "elegant," colors that please a person, shapes and sizes that seem appropriate.

Charles Spearman of England was the first to suggest directly that categories be used to stimulate the eduction of new ideas. The procedure proposed can be diagrammed with a wheel, where the hub represents a problem and the spokes represent any set of categories. An illustration using Aristotle's categories to find ways to develop a better mousetrap follows.

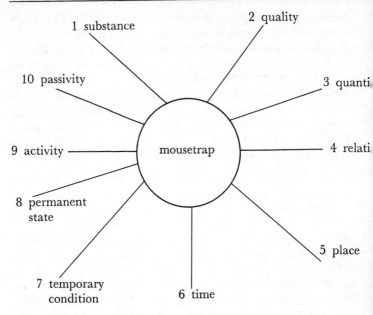

Educing Correlates to a Mousetrap by using Aristotle's Categories
In following the procedure the inventor would ask:

(1) Of what substance should the mousetrap be made? Wood? Tin? Plastic? Rubber?

(2) What qualities should it have? Soft? Hard? Round? Smooth?

(3) Should it be designed so that large quantities can readily be made?

(4) How will it relate to other things? How much will it cost? Will it be used in the home, office or warehouse?

(5) Where will it be put? On the floor? Against the wall? In a mouse's hole?

(6) Is it needed now? Will the demand last or be temporary?

(7) Will it have moving parts that will need to be adjusted?

(8) What parts will wear out? How long should it last?

(9) What action will the mousetrap make? Will it kill or just trap its mouse? If it kills the mouse, how will it do it?

(10) What is to be done to this mousetrap? Will it be packaged for sale? Will any of them be shipped a long way, as to India? Can it be put in place easily?

Aristotle would say that in asking these questions and others derived from the same categories, we have asked all the questions about a mousetrap that it is useful to ask. Without agreeing completely with this statement, we can still agree that an inventor who educes such a variety of correlates to any problem will have a good chance of developing some new ideas.

Educing the New by Rejecting or Questioning the Old. Creative thinkers are always in demand, and so few of them can be found that continuous efforts are made to teach young thinkers to be creative. To do this, the forces of convention and habit must be overcome. Given the idea "up," most people educe the word "down"; from "hot" they educe "cold"; from "work," "play." The dollar sign ($) brings to mind the word "dollar," and the symbols 5 x 5 makes one think of 25. Parents try to teach their children to do things in accordance with standards of correctness that are often set by tradition. Almost everyone has learned to dress, eat properly, and to drive his car in accordance with custom and law. A person learns to strike a nail with a hammer rather than with a shoe. He uses scissors to cut cloth, a watch to tell time. Doctors learn to give patients the proper medicine. Builders learn, from more experienced men, how to construct buildings that will not fall down. People in general follow the "proper" way of doing things as determined by established practice. Finally, their minds develop a "mental set" that keeps them within the bounds of habit. Alternatives do not occur to them. As an example, articles were made for many years in either black or white. Such things as umbrellas, telephones, printer's ink, and automobiles were always black. Such articles as men's shirts, towels, bed sheets, and paper were always white. Now, because some people had unconventional ideas about color, there is no unwritten law that anything *must* be black or white.

People who are too much dominated by custom, habit, or accepted practice seldom have any original ideas. A common technique of stimulating these people to become creative thinkers is to refuse their conventional answers and send them back to do their work over again. There are two well-known examples of this kind of training.

A famous instance of training by rejecting the conventional is told by Nathaniel S. Shaler, author of scientific papers and books, who became professor of paleontology at the Lawrence Scientific School of Harvard, and later its dean. Louis Agassiz administered the training. As a student, Shaler was applying for admission to Agassiz' laboratory. He was given an examination that included, with science, Latin, Greek, German, and French. Then Agassiz brought him a small fish saying that without reading or talking to others, and without damaging the specimen, he should examine it carefully. Shaler looked the fish over for an hour but when he felt ready to report he could not get Agassiz to question him. Time passed with no mark of attention from the professor. After a while, Shaler decided that some kind of game was involved. Carefully he went to work to examine the fish in every possible way. He found many things he had not suspected. Finally, after spending seven full days examining this one small fish, he was allowed to report. Agassiz talked with him. Feeling full of information, Shaler began a long explanation but after a few minutes Agassiz got up with the brief comment, "That is not right." Walking away, he left Shaler to spend another seven days of ten hours each on the same specimen. Feeling that Agassiz wanted to see if he could do hard continuous work, independent of the guidance of a teacher, Shaler, discarding all of his old notes, began again at the beginning. He now realized that he was learning to make original observations. This aroused him. Finally, at the end of a week, when the period was over, Shaler had results which, he said, surprised him and satisfied Agassiz.

A somewhat similar case was reported by Charles F. Kettering when he was in charge of research for General Motors. Kettering, who had difficulty in finding creative talent, tried in the following way to teach originality to one of his young engineers. He gave the man a handful of metal shavings, telling him to examine them carefully. The engineer identified the metals involved, got together some references dealing with those metals, and turned in his report. Kettering refused to accept it saying that he already knew the metals involved and could find his own references. He told the young man again to examine the shavings. After a little more work of the kind required in college, a second report was written which also was rejected. Finally, the idea penetrated the mind of Kettering's assistant that he was to examine the shavings until he found there something not described in the books. He then took a long time to examine the shavings. His next report, however, included observations that resulted in a new piston ring for automobiles that lasted three times as long as previous rings.

A famous example of rejecting the conventional way is found in a legend about Alexander the Great. The pole of a certain wagon had been fastened to the yoke with bark tied in an intricate knot. An oracle declared that anyone who could untie this knot would become the ruler of all Asia. Many tried, but all failed. Many were soldiers with swords at their sides, but they tried to untie the knot in the expected way. When Alexander the Great appeared, however, he did not attempt to untie the knot; he drew his sword and cut it.

Inventors and other creative thinkers "cut the knot" by ignoring tradition. They do things in some way other than the traditional way. One example is that of Leo Hendrik Baekeland, inventor of Bakelite. Plastics that were too soluble and softened easily under heat, had already been made. All the earlier patents indicated that plastic could be formed only if acids were used as condensing agents in temperatures below 212° F. Baekeland disregarded both of these accepted practices. He used bases for condensing agents and worked with high temperatures. The result was a harder and more durable plastic.

Eduction from a chance Base. William Perkins, in attempting to make synthetic quinine, was getting negative results from analine and various chemicals such as sulfuric acid. One day, he was throwing out an oily sludge, left over from his experiment, when he noticed that it had a purple color. This color, attracting his attention, led to new eductions. He tried the substance out as a dye with great success.

Charles Goodyear was trying to discover a method of vulcanizing rubber. For years he had been disappointed in all of his experiments. Finally, one day he was boiling rubber mixed with sulphur in the hope that this process would produce the result he had sought for so long. He had no success. Then, accidentally, a blob of the material fell on the stove and hardened. This accident became the basis of new and successful eductions, leading to a practical method of vulcanization.

So many great discoveries have been eductions from chance occurrences that this sort of discovery has been called "chance

within a context." The context calls for a man with the knowledge to recognize the significance of the gift that chance has
given him. Goodyear had not thought of spilling his rubber
mixture on the hot stove, but, when chance did that for him,
he was quick to see the importance of what had happened.

So often has chance presented a favorable basis for creative
eductions that various devices have been developed to secure
its assistance. These devices operate on the same basic idea as
the wheel, used with Aristotle's categories to design an improved
mousetrap. The base for the eductions is determined in some
chance way. One very old and familiar technique is that one of
opening the Bible to some chance verse and looking there for
the solution of one's problems. Dictionaries and catalogues have
been used in place of the Bible, with individual words, or paired
words from different places, serving as the source of eductions.
Another device is to list the parts of an object and then educe
ideas from the relationship of the parts to the whole; or one
may take a high level concept and relate it to all the subordinate
ideas ranging under it. The essence of this method is to seek
novel ideas by attempting to educe them from a novel base.

In examining these chance creations we find the heart of
original thinking, which is to put together in a significant way
ideas that have always before been separate.

Eduction and Relaxation. The value of relaxation in creativity can be seen best by comparing relaxation with work.
Work involves rejecting all the possible alternatives in favor of
the one activity that will get the job done. The worker must
resist the temptation of distraction. He must refuse to stop
and rest, to talk of last night's recreation, or to plan a picnic.
After he is well-trained these rejections become automatic, so
that distractions are immediately put aside.

Concentration is a state of mind which illustrates again the
focusing of all one's energies to the exclusion of daydreams,
fancies and improbabilities. Concentration, the state of paying
unwavering attention to one's work, is eagerly sought by good
workmen. It involves doing the appointed task without mind
wandering in search of novelties.

When one relaxes, on the other hand, he has in mind no
definite purpose or objective. The mind of the daydreamer is
open to any idea that floats in. He rejects nothing since he has

no reason to reject anything. The daydreamer can entertain any kind of idea no matter how novel or strange.

Significant ideas, however, do not seem to come to the permanently idle. Nothing can come out of the mind that has not already been in it. Only new combinations of old ideas bring creative insight. Therefore, creative thinkers are almost always hard workers as well as good students. Usually they know all there is to know about the field in which they do their original work. They also have periods of relaxation which are sometimes very productive. In each of the following illustrations of creativity we will find periods of relaxation following the accumulation of knowledge.

Archimedes (287-212 B.C.) was the greatest scientist of his day, a mathematician and physicist who invented the lever and the screw. His friend, King Hieron of Syracuse, having ordered a crown made of gold suspected the goldsmith of having used an alloy. King Hieron asked Archimedes to determine, without melting the crown, whether base metals had been used. Archimedes did not know how to do this thing, but he did know a great many things. Just how long he worked on the problem we do not know, but one day when bathing he noticed that the water rose as his body displaced it. In a flash he saw that a certain weight of gold would replace less water than the same weight of silver, because it was smaller. He had found the key to the solution of his problem.

Copernicus (1473-1543) provides us with another famous example. Born in Prussian Poland, he learned astronomy at the University of Krakow and studied mathematics in Italy before returning to East Prussia, where he became canon of the cathedral. He had been taught that the earth was stationary at the center of the universe, with the sun and stars moving around it. The explanation was neither simple nor satisfactory, but it was generally accepted. One day, Copernicus, relaxed and daydreaming, was in a small boat floating quietly near the bank of the river. Chancing to look aside he had the illusion that the bank was moving while his boat remained stationary. Suddenly he realized that the same kind of illusion might cause the belief that the earth remained still while the sun moved. He experimented with reversing the generally accepted theory by assuming that the sun stood still while the earth, with its planets, revolved around it. Thus, the Copernican theory of astronomy was founded.

Since some people believe that these ancient stories are fictitious, it may be well to support them with modern examples that are well authenticated.

Henri Poincaré, one of the great mathematicians of France, was deeply interested in how his mind worked. In the chapter "Mathematical Creation" of his book *The Foundations of Science* he states that he believes that the mind does "subconscious work." He observes that in making inventions the mind must select new combinations of associations from among an infinite number. A good mind rejects most of the possible combinations without even being aware of doing so. Poincaré says creativity consists in selecting from among the possibilities the small number of useful combinations. Invention involves discernment and choice. The associations wanted are those which, having been stored in the mind as strangers, are immediately recognized as significantly joined when associated.

Explaining further how he believes inventions are often brought about by subconscious work, Poincaré gives these examples. For fifteen days, he says, he worked to prove that there could not be any such thing as Fuchsian functions in mathematics. Then one night, contrary to custom, he was kept awake by drinking black coffee. Ideas flooded through his mind so that by next morning he had established a class of Fuchsian functions which were ready to be written down. Later, at Coutances, while making a geologic journey for the school of mines, at the very moment he put his foot on the step to enter a bus, the idea flashed on his mind that the methods he had been using with Fuchsian functions were identical with those of non-Euclidean geometry. He did not even stop the conversation he was having, but still, the insight was so firmly fixed in his mind that he was able to verify it when his trip was over. On other occasions, when he was in military service, the solution to another mathematical problem flashed into his mind as he was walking along the street. He did not even try to work out all the details immediately, but, after his military service was completed, he found that he still had in mind all the elements needed to put together his new discovery.

A contemporary example of creative insight coming during

a period of relaxation is given by Dr. Albert Schweitzer, the missionary-philosopher of Africa. Dr. Schweitzer had become discouraged for the future of civilization. The attitude of the East was negative, whereas the affirmative attitude of the West lacked an ethical foundation. On what philosophy could a sound civilization be based? Having formulated his problem, Schweitzer tried for months to find a solution. Finally, he had to go a hundred and sixty miles upstream, on a small steamer towing a barge. Late on the third day of his enforced idleness, at the very moment when at sunset they were making their way through a herd of hippopotamuses there flashed upon his mind, "unforseen and unsought" the idea of "Reverence for Life," which he then made the central theme of his philosophy.

Cases of invention such as those given above have led to a formula for creativity that includes the following five steps: *First,* become critically aware of a problem. This usually provides the motivation required to organize one's efforts. *Second,* learn all that is known about the subject as did Archimedes, Copernicus, Poincaré, and Schweitzer. With such preparation chance experiences may have significant referents. *Third,* allow a period of incubation or relaxation. *Fourth,* wait for illumination. In the matter of illumination is found the difference between the inventive mind and one that is not so original. As Gauss, the mathematician, said, he got his ideas "not by dint of effort, but by the grace of God." *Fifth,* verify, or develop the insight by careful work.

Eduction with Visual Aids. It is possible to imagine things but these imaginings are not as real as the objects we see about us in the actual world. Neither the imagination nor the memory can produce objects that are as clear and distinct as those reaching us through our senses.

Visual aids help us to realize ideas fully. "One picture is worth ten thousand words." Novels and short stories contain all the plots that have appeared on the stage; but, as Schopenhauer declared, one might as well dress without a mirror as live without attending the theater.

The improved sharpness, color, and atmosphere given to ideas by visual representation have proved useful in creative thinking. Sculptors make models of their projected works.

Architects make scale drawings of the structures they plan to build, often drawing the landscape as well to get a clearer idea of the building in its surroundings. Engineers "mock-up" the new cars they are designing. No manufacturer would think of tooling a plant for a new automobile until the car had been studied in model form. One of the basic requirements for apprentices in many trades is the ability to read blueprints. Such drawings help in the comprehension of complex machines. The imagination can picture a whole machine; but, when the details of the parts are under consideration a blueprint is needed to hold the attention. There have been men who could play chess blindfolded, but for the average player seeing the board is a necessity.

Photography helps in a thousand ways to create new things. Photographs show processes going on under water, in intense heat, and inside machines where the human eye cannot see. Cameras with electronic attachments take a thousand photographs in a second showing exactly how an operation is taking place. Cameras go along with experimental satellites to bring back information from outer space.

Since visualization is so important in understanding many operations it is not surprising to find visual aids used to create new situations. Executives have been known to attack business problems as if they were playing a game of chess, clearing their desks and putting out objects to represent the various factors in their problems. By moving these objects around, they get new ideas of the forces with which they are contending. A specific example of this practice is the use of templets, or small models properly proportioned, to lay out an office or factory. With scaled objects to represent each object the contents of a room can be moved until the best arrangement is discovered.

A very famous use of visual aids is the Periodic Table, which is used in the search for new chemical elements. The table indicates that elements of specific atomic weights with a particular arrangement of nucleus and shell will be found. Prediction made on the basis of this table first led to the discovery of gallium and germanium, and are now being used to hunt for elements 104 through 108. A helpful factor in the search for new elements is that all elements, both those known and those sought, can now be diagrammed. These diagrams sharpen the concept of the element being hunted.

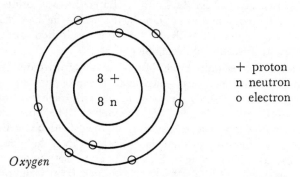

+ proton
n neutron
o electron

Oxygen

Associational Possibilities in Higher-Level Concepts. All high-level concepts have the function of bringing together things that under many circumstances would be so widely separated that one would never think of combining them. The concept of science, for instance, is at such a high level of abstraction that it can bring together many unlike percepts. The sting of a drop of acid on the skin, the reflexes of a mouse, and the trajectory of a bullet fired from a gun are all parts of science.

It follows directly that every original thinker should acquaint himself with the accumulated knowledge in his field. Some years ago it was common to debate the value of such knowledge for inventors. It was frequently assumed that education decreased originality. But this idea, resulting from a confusion of the concepts of education with indoctrination, has proven false. Thomas Edison has sometimes been considered an example of an uneducated genius. But he was tutored by his mother, a school-teacher, and always considered his education inadequate. In his younger years he regarded Faraday's *Experimental Researches in Electricity* as his Bible. Before he built his Menlo Park laboratory, he used the Princeton University laboratory where he conferred often with the professor of physics, Dr. C. F. Brackett. When he had his own laboratory, it was Edison's practice to employ well-trained young university scientists as his assistants, and his library of scientific books was immense.

Alexander Graham Bell, inventor of the telephone, was the

son of the inventor of "visible speech" with which the deaf were taught to speak. Bell was educated at Edinburgh University and at University College in London. Later, he was professor of Vocal Physiology at Boston University, where he had many contacts with scientists, both in his own institution and at Massachusetts Institute of Technology.

Whenever one examines the life of a major inventor, one finds him well informed in his own field. Inventors are formally trained, or else, by study or association with highly trained men, acquire the information for themselves. They pay close attention to the higher-level concepts in their field, as well as to the percepts involved in their daily work. In fact, the greatest innovators, like Newton and Einstein, have been among the best trained men. Sir Isaac Newton graduated from Cambridge and held a professorship there. Albert Einstein studied at Zurich and Prague. In 1914 he became director of the Kaiser Wilhelm Institute, and later he became the head of the School of Mathematics at the Institute for Advanced Study at Princeton University.

Lower-level concepts relate percepts that are close together in experience and usually produce knowledge of immediate practical usefulness. Higher-level concepts bring together the distantly related theoretical knowledge that is difficult to apply but that once understood may "move the world," as Archimedes said he could do with his lever, and as Einstein did, metaphorically, with his Theory of Relativity.

Culture is a storehouse of higher-level concepts that, ingeniously applied, are capable of solving most of the problems that emerge from everyday living.

Eduction by a Group. Since creative thinking can be stimulated by new and unexpected combinations of ideas, it seems obvious that it can sometimes be prompted by the combination of various minds. A group technique that has frequently been used to produce originality in advertising, management, and science, has been called "brainstorming." This technique, said to have been devised by Alex Osborn, requires a group of approximately twelve people. They are given a problem on which they are asked to express any ideas that come to them. The rules prohibit judging the new ideas till later. The wildest ideas that come to mind are to be proposed. There should be cross-association, with one person picking up and expanding on an idea suggested by another person. A great many ideas are sought. Embarrassment at expressing one's uncensored, and perhaps foolish, thoughts must be eliminated in a free atmosphere of people having more or less the same status. Participants, however, should have different backgrounds to provide the greatest variety of ideas.

Although it is said that creative individuals are too individualistic to be good "organization men," they have frequently worked in groups. Inventors have often joined forces in the research teams of large corporations and in government work. Patent statistics suggest that today corporation employees are producing more inventions than they once did. In the United States the proportion of corporation patents rose from 18% in 1900 to 58% in 1955. In England such patents rose from 13% in 1913 to 68% in 1955.

THE PROBLEM OF DEFINITION

The problem of definition is to bring the accumulated knowledge of all time to bear on a particular problem. Knowledge reduces more difficulties and saves more labor than any device that man has ever discovered. Problems, however, must be related to general knowledge by adequate definitions before we can know the proper prescription for a particular situation. In order to understand this need for definition, we must know how the human race has organized and stored its experience.

The Organization of Knowledge. A person can use his own practical experience without much thought, and for some people this seems to be enough. Such personal experience gives us our sense of reality and helps us in competing with other men by providing us with secrets which no one else has. Furthermore, once we have this practical experience it can be used without giving it another thought.

But the trouble with practical experience is that it does not reach very far. One man can recall only a limited number of things. For thousands of years other men have been accumulating experiences and storing knowledge. A man must learn to find this knowledge and use it.

A simple example of the use of stored knowledge can be taken from a common experience. Suppose one sees a boy running in from the yard with blood on his hands, face, and sleeves. A quick examination indicates that the blood comes from his nose, and we form a concept of nosebleed. There are various kinds of nosebleed—those due to arteriosclerosis, to liver disease, to high blood pressure, to injury. In this case, the nosebleed is probably due to some physical injury. This hypothesis must be tested by applying an established generalization indicating what to do for nosebleeds due to physical injury. Such a generalization can be found in a medical encyclopedia where we read that the patient should be placed with his head and shoulders elevated and that he should breathe through the mouth. Further suggestions may be found if the remedy given above does not help. If the nosebleed stops, the hypothesis previously made can be considered correct.

If we wish we can write a formal syllogism on the nosebleed test, as follows: In all cases of nosebleed due to injury the patient should be kept quiet with his head and shoulders elevated and should breathe through the mouth. This case is a case of nosebleed due to injury. Therefore the patient should be treated as described.

If the nosebleed does not stop in a reasonable time, it is probable that our minor premise is untrue and that this is not a case of nosebleed from ordinary injury. It may be necessary to go all the way back to examine the underlying facts again before a new hypothesis can be formed. In medical cases of this kind, certainly in those that are more complex, a doctor is brought in to carry the major burden of the thinking, but the presence of the doctor does not change the essential nature of the process. We have in this illustration an example of how all the world's stored knowledge is put to use.

Types and Methods of Definition. Once we have established the percept of the boy with the bloody nose, the abstract generalized statement representing many nosebleeds is a definition. The task of a definition is to establish both the meaning and the boundaries of a concept. A logical definition clarifies meaning by placing a concept in a class, at the same time that it differentiates it from other members of the group. (A loblolly is a pine tree of the Southern United States that has thick bark and long needles; its wood is coarse and inferior). This kind of definition is called a *Connotative definition* since to the simple meaning of a word it adds the wider suggestion of class membership. The connotative definition is to be distinguished from the use of connotation to indicate the emotional suggestions that accompany a word.

There are five general rules of connotative definitions which enable us to relate our ideas to the general store of knowledge. The first is that the definition should be in the terms of the nearest larger recognizable class, with adequate differentiating data. For instance, *deduction,* which we have examined, is defined as a type of reasoning different from other types of reasoning in that the information about specific instances is derived from general principles. The larger the class referred to in the definition the more certain it is to be recognized, but, also, the greater is the work of giving adequate differentia. If *deduction* had been defined as a "series of statements," instead of as a type of reasoning, it would require much effort to differentiate it from other series of statements.

The second rule is that the definitions should not be circular, that is, the concept in question should not be used in its own definition. Do not define a sleeping-powder as a powder that puts one to sleep.

The third rule is that a definition give the essential characteristics, and only those, of the term being defined. To define a dog as an animal that is gentle and kind is inadequate, since the adjectives are not essential to the proper classification of the dog.

The fourth rule is that a definition should not be negative, merely telling what a concept is not. It is insufficient to define *heroism* as an act that is not cowardly.

The fifth rule is that the definition should be expressed in language that can be understood.

Any concept that has been properly classified inductively can be given a connotative definition. Many things have never been classified and fitted into a general system of knowledge.

In consequence, two forms of definition have been devised for
such cases. One of them is called *nominal* definition and the
other a *denotative* definition. A *nominal* definition is the simplest
because it uses synonyms to make the meaning clear. For instance, the Winston Dictionary defines practice (in part) as
"habit, exercise, usage." *Denotative Definition,* the second type,
attempts to make the meaning of a concept clear by giving
examples. In Webster's *New International Dictionary* a quad-
rangle is defined as, "A square or quadrangular enclosure or
court, esp., as in some English schools, when surrounded by
buildings."

In attempting to understand a subject one begins, if possible,
with a connotative definition which places the subject within
classified knowledge. After this, if he wishes to study the matter
further he may refer to the Dewey Decimal system of the
Library of Congress system of classifying subjects. In the
Dewey Decimal system there are ten main classifications to
which a numbering system has been assigned, as follows:

000-099 General works—Encyclopedias, bibliographies, peri-
odicals.
100-199 Philosophy, psychology, ethics.
200-299 Religion and mythology.
300-399 Sociology—economics, civics, education, vocations.
400-499 Philology—language.
500-599 Science—mathematics, physics, chemistry, biology,
zoology, botany.
600-699 Useful Arts—medicine, engineering, agriculture,
radio, aviation.
700-799 Fine Arts—painting, music, photography.
800-899 Literature—novels, plays, poetry, criticism.
900-999 History, geography, biography, travel.

These ten classes are further divided. The Useful Arts, for
instance, are subdivided as follows:
600 General Technology
610 Medicine
620 Engineering
630 Agriculture
640 Home Economics
650 Business

660 Chemical Technology
670 Manufactures
680 Industrial Training
690 Building

Each of these divisions is further divided, and when the classification becomes very fine, decimals are used.

To find a particular book the system of index classification will also be used. This is sometimes called artificial classification because it has nothing to do with the association of ideas or the relationships of knowledge, and is based exclusively on the alphabet. Such disparate subjects as the Laguna Dam in Arizona and the city Lahore, in Pakistan, may be found side by side in an index. The value of alphabetical indexing, however, is well-known. With such an index one can trace down any item of knowledge that has been stored away in book or library.

Definition in Law—an Illustration. The rights of men are defined in the codified law. These rights are grouped, forming concepts, and named, as all concepts are named, to aid concise communication and clear thought. First degree murder and manslaughter are examples of such concepts.

"Murder in the second degree," or "manslaughter," names a concept which represents killing without a premeditated intention; as in passion, or by failing to control a dangerous dog or angry bull which one owns, or by carelessly allowing too many people to sit in the front seat of an automobile.

When murder has been observed, or has left evidence observable by the senses, such evidence consists of percepts. These are reported to the grand jury which relates the percepts to the already formed concepts of the codified law. If the grand jury decides that the evidence is sufficient, some person is indicted and charged with the crime.

When the case comes to court a jury is selected to examine the percepts, that is, to determine the facts. The defendant and the State have attorneys to protect their rights. The judge guides the case through the court and makes sure, if possible, that the evidence is related to the act for which the defendant was indicted.

The decision of the jury asserts that an act of a particular description was, or was not, committed. The judge sentences a guilty person guided by a syllogism, as follows: All persons guilty of first degree murder shall be executed. This man is guilty of first degree murder. Therefore this man shall be executed.

An interesting aspect of the law is that it is a "living discipline." As new ways of murder are discovered, by radiation, or by flying one's victim high in the air without an oxygen mask, the acts by which the deeds are done must be examined and fitted into pre-existing legal concepts, or to new concepts which are created.

Summary. Definition is a necessary step in the utilization of knowledge. Experience comes to us in percepts, which we can share to some extent by description, but which we quickly classify into concepts, where we find the first level of widely-shared knowledge. These concepts are defined to give them clarity and names with which to relate them to other concepts. Generalizations, or laws, describe uniform aspects of classified concepts pointing to applications of knowledge. Any bit of knowledge the human race possesses is available, stored away in libraries by alphabetical classification, for the solution of any problem, by any person.

PROBLEMS OF CHOICE

Some people would "rather be right than president," others would rather be president than right, while still others never have the choice to make. In brief, choices are personal.

Choice is required when possible solutions to a problem are mutually exclusive. The same processes that characterize all thinking will be used here. In making choices, motivation must be recognized, facts classified, inferences made, and conclusions verified. The uniqueness of choice-problems lies in the fact that some of the arguments will be weighted by personal experience. The verification of the conclusion, therefore, will be determined partly by personal preferences. No man should marry a woman he does not like merely for logical reasons.

Personal Experience. Experience begins with sensory responses. Simple sensation brings us information that is pleasant, indifferent, or unpleasant. People usually agree in judging sugar sweet, iron heavy, and steam hot. But such agreements are seldom complete. Some people like sugar in their coffee and some do not. Some people like weather warm, some like it cold. So common are these individual preferences that disagreements as to what is desirable are almost as common as agreements.

People even change their memories in individual ways. A person likes to review pleasant experiences and not think too long about unpleasant ones. He gradually builds up quite a store of information which supports his ego. These data will obviously be different selections from those remembered by his friend who unconsciously selects memories to support his own ego.

These differences lead still further to the building of personal precedents. When one decision is made, a dozen more are likely to follow. The decision to go to college brings almost automatically the decision to buy books, pay tuition, secure lodging, and study. As decisions accumulate, people form ideas of their own personalities and follow the role they have established for themselves. This is most easily illustrated by the way people dress. Some dress like members of a teen-age gang, some as school teachers, cowboys, executives, bankers or preachers. Many decisions follow in the same way, the person acting as he imagines a person of his occupation and character should act.

Shared Experience. To this accumulation of personal experience we must add shared or vicarious experience. Shared experience and personal experience become so intermingled that it is impossible to separate them. When an individual sets up goals for himself, these goals are determined partly by what is considered desirable in some segment of society. A juvenile delinquent, a beatnik, or a criminal is not an isolated nonconformist, but a person who is conforming to the ideals of his own social group. A young man might, for example, set up one or more of the following goals:

To graduate from a university
To marry a sensible girl
To rear children
To be healthy
To find a good job
To be strong and virile
To be sensible and conservative
To read the one hundred best books

Such goals, which represent choices, are fixed partly by

personal preference and partly by social pressure. Even in such a complex field as ethics, where there is much disagreement, there is considerable uniform pressure based on shared experience. H. L. Mencken, in his *Treatise on Right and Wrong*, says (page 7) "The five fundamental prohibitions of the Decalogue —those leveled at murder, theft, trespass, adultery and false witness—are found in every moral system ever heard of and seem to be universally supported by human opinion."

Shared experience influences many individual choices and decisions. It operates through a respect for customs, etiquette, and law, as well as through knowledge acquired in books. It is the force of custom that makes it unthinkable to eat with one's knife. It is custom that determines that women may kiss each other but men may not. It is custom that permits people to wear bathing suits on a beach but not in church. It is custom that excuses a person for telling "white lies," such as "How well you are looking!" Laws add a final imperative to shared experience in determining choices. Few people choose to disregard the law and go to jail.

Generally, the higher the abstraction about which information is shared, the greater the agreement. We find the greatest disagreement and the greatest evidence of choice in individual tastes. Nature has fortunately arranged that although all men admire feminine beauty, it is not often that two men fall violently in love with one woman.

One of the main problems of choice is that of separating the personal from the impersonal evidence. A person should ask himself what choice would be made by a robot in the identical circumstances. Then he should determine what weight in the decision is properly accorded to his own preferences. This is what Socrates had in mind in making his famous declaration, "Know thyself."

Selecting a friend or a wife or an occupation has in it a big element of personal preference. Selecting an investment is better done on a more impersonal basis.

A good choice is satisfying to the chooser as well as to others who are affected by it. Young people make choices that affect their lives many years later under altered conditions. Older people are often in a position where their choices affect the happiness of other people.

In objective choosing the thinking is the same as that in definition. In subjective choosing, dependent upon one's personal preferences, it is often hard to determine the facts. It would simplify many personal decisions if the facts supporting the preferences could be recorded. Poor decisions in regard to money are often made through ignorance of personal circumstances. People buy things they cannot afford; others miss good opportunities to buy needed articles or to travel, because they do not have a clear idea of their financial condition. A simple bookkeeping system would improve the financial decisions of many people.

It would also be helpful if an individual kept other types of records—his blood type, records of illnesses, school and college grades, jobs held and wages earned, honors won, and recommendations. An indexed record of all such personal data would provide solid information for many personal decisions.

After one has marshaled the pertinent data, including an estimate of his own motivation, the next step might be to obtain advice and counseling. In schools and colleges, where many people have somewhat similar adjustment problems, professional advisers are provided. For others there are friends who will at least try to help one to objectify his problems. There is an art in asking for and listening to advice. Many people are afraid of advice because it may go counter to their desires by calling into question their personal emphasis on certain facts. These are the very reasons why advice is helpful. It is often wise to get advice from various sources but not to feel impelled to follow it just because it has been asked for and given. Advice should be followed only when it is convincing and pertinent.

In business the conference technique helps the executive both by aiding in objectifying decisions and by contributing relevant information. Faulty judgment can ruin a business.

When a choice, or decision, has been made, it should be tested. There are three ways of testing conclusions; two of them are applicable to all thinking, whereas the third is applicable only where personal preferences are concerned. The universally used methods are those of consistency and the empirical test of application. The personal preference test indicates whether the decision gives satisfaction to the person doing the thinking.

The test of consistency is based on the fact that all verified knowledge is related, and consequently, any conclusion should be consistent with all the facts known. The test is not always adequate because in some problems many facts are still unavailable when a decision must be reached. Nevertheless, it is discouraging to find a proposed conclusion apparently inconsistent with some established facts, whereas it is always reassuring to find them consistent.

The empirical test of application should be used quickly to save time in matters of little importance and delayed as long as possible in cases where the choice is irreparable.

A choice is of comparatively little importance in buying a pair of shoes, and it does not pay to gather facts and weigh them endlessly. Buy the shoes, and if they do not satisfy you, try another brand. So with hundreds of little choices in everyday life. If the decision is minor, do something and get it over with. Time, too, is worth something. But as decisions grow in importance, it becomes necessary to apply all the rules of consistency known before testing the conclusion by use. This should be done only when it is necessary to act.

Choices which have grave consequences should be studied carefully before a decision is reached. When a person gets married he can never return to the same point for a second try. He may return to his single status in the eyes of the law but only as a changed person. When war is declared, it is never possible to go back to the same point in history, with all the conditions as they were, to decide again. In business there are many choices that change things irrevocably. In fact, the very nature of choice is that, if the decision is wrong, the consequences can never be completely escaped.

The test of personal preference should be often applied but seldom followed. An executive when making decisions that should be objective, ought still to know the bearing of his feelings. One of the main difficulties of decision-making in business is that the right decision is often emotionally difficult. Friends should not be favored, relatives employed, or favorites advanced for emotional reasons. It has been said that executive success is as much dependent upon "good guts" as upon good thinking. Here the resistance to personal preferences is required.

In selecting clothes, hobbies, vacation sites, friends, and

occupations, personal preferences should be frankly recognized. Of what good is a friend if he is not liked, of a vacation if it is not enjoyed, of a recreation if it is not found pleasant? In all cases where winning personal satisfaction is the paramount issue the test of personal preference should be applied. It is a happy situation when all three ways of testing a conclusion agree.

PROBLEMS OF PROCEDURE

All how-to-do-it problems have the common factor of time. One thing must be done first, others must follow. The assembly line in any factory illustrates this.

Thinking has been described as doing things mentally in order to test out the steps before doing them physically. There are many steps which must be performed in proper sequence in doing all but the simplest things. It takes careful thinking to go through these steps mentally before the first step is taken physically. A house should be completely planned on paper, with every part specified, before the carpenter goes to work.

The elements of thinking—percepts, concepts and generalizations—are the same in how-to-do-it problems as in other problems, but there is a difference in the use of inferences. In many kinds of thinking it is possible to develop and test one hypothesis at a time. But in problems of procedure, because a series of operations must be planned at one time, and each proposed operation is a hypothesis, multiple hypotheses must be established before the work starts and others as the work progresses. These hypotheses must be tested as well as can be done without the benefit of controlled conditions. This results in a loss of precision that takes how-to-do-it problems out of the realm of science into the area of skilled workmanship. Some help is obtained from the fact that sciences support the how-to-do-it skills. The science of physics underlies engineering, several sciences provide a background for surgery, and chemistry supports pharmaceutics. The sciences provide many facts that enable the technician to work with fewer hypotheses at one time and thus help to clarify his thinking.

Any problem of procedure can be divided for examination into four categories, as follows: (1) objective; (2) strategy; (3) tactics; and (4) skill. This order proceeds from the highest level of abstract concepts, the objective, down to the skill of the individual, which is largely on the perceptual level.

Objective.   An objective is usually clear in inverse order to its degree of abstraction. For instance, the objective in World Wars I and II was given as "making the world safe for democracy." This objective has seemed continually more desirable, but just what the objective requires in the way of action is not clear. The World Court, the League of Nations, and the United Nations grew out of this concept, but the procedures must be subject to development if the objective is to be reached.

Definite objectives are needed in the operation of a business. A corporation may be organized to manufacture a particular group of products or to supply a service. Its objectives should enable answers to be given to such questions as: Who will profit by these operations? Is expansion to be sought? Will there be an increasing demand for the products of the company?

Definite objectives are needed even for very simple activities such as the building of a table lamp. Will the lamp be used as a utility or for a decoration? If it is to be used as a utility, will it be used for reading or handicraft work? How much light is needed and what shadows will be cast?

Strategy.   Strategy is an over-all plan for working toward the objective. In it there are many operations to be considered, those compulsory, advisable, and contradictory to the proposed objective. In making war, the strategist organizes all the military, political, economic, and psychological forces and directs them toward victory. In peacetime, military strategy must be aimed to keep the support of friendly nations and to develop, train, and equip sea, air, and land troops. It must be used to protect the homeland and its industrial base so that the country will have mobilization schedules prepared, at any moment, for war.

Business strategy is usually called *administration* and the administrator is responsible for using all of a corporation's resources to meet competition. He must subdivide the task into operations, such as engineering, merchandising, and production, and see to it that each division is properly equipped and directed. He must develop the principles or policies on which the business operates, for example, the principle of simplicity, eliminating unnecessary operations; the principle of function-alization, building the business around functions rather than around individual men; and the principle of centralization, giving the operation centralized executive control. In manufacturing automobiles it is the task of strategy to determine whether it is feasible to produce a particular car; will it be air-cooled, water-cooled, or perhaps a turbine engine be used. There is a need for strategy in building even a simple table lamp. The strategy of lamp making requires a survey of the various materials that might be used, the investment of time and money required as well as the machines and tools needed. Strategy requires the organization of an activity within an environment. It is an over-all plan that takes in all aspects of a task and its operational surroundings.

Tactics.   Tactics deals with the parts of a how-to-do-it problem rather than with the whole. It is concerned with the battle rather than the war. The military tactician studies the use of the phalanx by Alexander, the handling of his legions by Caesar, and the techniques of battle used by Napoleon. The tactician studies the various uses of artillery, infantry, tanks, and planes in battle. His problems include communications during fighting, the uses of reserves in action, and the management of supplies. The tactics of business, dealing with the control of day-to-day activities, are usually termed *management*. Materials are purchased, tools maintained, and employees supervised. The manager is also interested in the skill and efficiency of the workman. Careful testing, interviewing, and placing employees where they will do their best work has become a major aspect of business tactics. In lamp making, tactics requires specifying a sequence of operations. It might, for instance, be as follows:
1. Cut the pieces to size
2. Sand the wooden parts
3. Fasten the parts together
4. Make the holes for the electric cord
5. Insert the pipe into the top of the lamp
6. Complete the sanding
7. Put on the finish
8. Assemble and wire

The actual operations should follow the tactical plan closely, particularly the time order, if the job is to be done efficiently.

Skill.   Skill is needed to perform an operation in a superior way. Skill is required to throw a curve in baseball, to operate a typewriter rapidly, or to sew a straight seam.

A soldier must have skill to have confidence in himself as a fighter. He must be able to take his rifle apart in the dark to clean it. He must be able to shoot straight. He needs training in the use of tools, weapons, and equipment because his skill may determine his survival.

In industry the skill of the individual worker is essential, or tools will be broken and material wasted. Industry continually finds it necessary to conduct training programs to improve the skills of the individual workman. Without some degree of skill, even a table lamp may never be completed in spite of the enthusiasm of a "do it yourself" operator. *Skill* can be defined as an organized group of habits which takes time to form. No workman becomes skilled overnight, but by organizing good work habits into a skilled performance he may eventually become a superior workman.

Summary. How-to-do-it problems have been broken down into the separate areas of objectives, strategy, tactics, and skill. The division has the advantage of calling attention to the different steps in order to see that each step is done properly. The common element in all how-to-do-it problems is time, and the making of plans is its most difficult aspect. The planning of consecutive steps before operations begin requires that a number of hypotheses be tested almost simultaneously. The plans are the hypotheses, and the way they work out is the test. The great difficulty of how-to-do-it thinking is that it must operate without experimental controls. Sometimes the reason for failure is difficult to pinpoint as when a good plan is ruined for lack of skill. When plans prove faulty they must be replaced by new ones, thus continuing the thinking process until the action is completed.

THE PROBLEM OF EXPLANATION— PHILOSOPHY AND SCIENCE

The General Problem of Explanation. The problem of explanation might be said to carry one to the end of thinking. Explanations follow the event to clarify solutions. Just as one is driven to original thinking if he has a problem, so he is urged to explain if he has solved a problem.

Things are explained by being related to other things that are already understood. Ancient astronomers who made many observations of the movements of the stars could only wonder why the heavenly bodies went on such strange journeys. Then Sir Isaac Newton learned that the movements of the stars, as well as of falling bodies on earth, responded to the same law of gravity. This discovery was a great step forward in understanding the universe.

The unique can be sensed but is not usually understood. Thus, we find the adolescent feeling that his problems are too individual to be generalized, crying "no one understands me." He knows no familiar laws or common notions that explain his experience. People stand before the famous Mona Lisa of Leonardo and wonder what the woman's enigmatic smile can mean. Attempts to understand the smile rely on common ideas. "She smiles with satisfaction at the thought that she is both rich and beautiful"; "She smiles that she may hold the attention of the man she admires, the great artist Leonardo."

Four common techniques are used to make strange things seem familiar. We identify them, by definition, with well known concepts, as when boys get into a fight with pocket knives and the newspaper explains the disturbance as a "Teen-age war." A second method is by covering the unique with a generalization as when a young sales clerk is reproved for arguing with a client by the statement, "Remember, the customer is always right." A third way of making the new seem familiar is by pointing out an analogy as when some one explains Einstein's Law of Relativity by describing trains on parallel tracks going in the same direction, and again in opposite directions. A fourth method of describing the unique in common terms is to give its cause or effects. This is done when an automobile stalls on the highway and the owner explains to the traffic officer that the car stalled because it ran out of gas.

If explanations are to be clear the higher-level concepts must be meaningful and relevant, the generalizations sound, the analogies truly similar in some way to the things explained, and the causes or effects properly established.

Explanation in Philosophy. Although explanations are made in every field of knowledge the task of explaining the abstruse things of life is the task of the philosopher and, to some extent, of the scientist. There was a time when philosophy included all thought so that every serious student called himself a philosopher. Immanuel Kant was the first to distinguish science from philosophy, and the word "scientist" appeared about fifty years after his death. As late as 1887, laboratory equipment such as test tubes and scales were sometimes catalogued as "philosophical instruments." But today there is a division of labor, even in thinking, leaving the group of professional philosophers relatively limited. Philosophy deals with problems that can be examined by pure reason; science with problems that can be explained by established facts; and religion with problems clarified by revealed knowledge. As revelation is not subject to analysis, religion is not a part of the subject matter of this book.

Philosophy includes explanations of many things that will help one in his everyday thinking. Philosophers are concerned that all concepts have meaning, consequently they are repeatedly interpreting such ideas as beauty, freedom, and justice in current terms. Old concepts relating to circumstances that have passed away are discarded. Generalizations must be consistent with each other in a system of integrated knowledge.

In making their explanations the philosophers have classified their problems. One such classification divides philosophy into methodology, metaphysics, and the theory of value. We will examine these in turn.

Methodology. Logic and epistemology are included in methodology. Since this book deals with the ways of attaining knowledge, which is logic, we need not here discuss it further. Epistemology is an examination of the ways of interpreting knowledge. Philosophers, in attempting to relate all knowledge, find themselves in somewhat the same position as did the blind men in examining the elephant. One of the blind men in feeling the tail of the elephant said the animal was like a big snake; another, feeling its leg, said the elephant was like a pillar holding up a building; another, feeling the side of the elephant, said the other blind men were wrong since the elephant was undoubtedly like the side of a house. Philosophers, taking all of the universe of knowledge for their province without yet knowing what all knowledge is, find themselves limited as were the blind men. One school of thought asserts that knowledge comes only through the senses. In the words of John Locke, "There is nothing in the mind which was not first in the senses." Another school holds that the mind contributes to knowledge certain essential ideas not obtained from experience. The nature of knowledge is considered by the realists to reflect an independent, objective universe. To the idealist the ideas brought forth by the mind are regarded as more real than the evidence of the senses. Plato, for example, considered ideas to be more permanent than the changing world in which we live. It is the task of epistemology to examine, and if possible reconcile, these various interpretations of the universe.

Metaphysics. Aristotle wrote a book on physics, after which he wrote another book that was called the "After Physics" or Metaphysics. The subject matter of the second book became identified with this meaningless title so that they are still joined even today. Metaphysics deals with the kind of truth about reality that can be proven by reason as contrasted to physics in which truth is established by experiment. The problems of metaphysics are divided into two groups: those of ontology in which knowledge is separated for analysis and those of cosmology in which knowledge is put together and organized. In ontology we find an examination of the fundamental categories of existence, among which are time and space. In cosmology, on the other hand, the central problem is the order found in nature as indicated by all available knowledge of the time resulting in a unified conception of the universe.

Theory of Value. The theory of value is subdivided into the study of the good with the means of realizing it, which is ethics; and the study of the beautiful with the means of expressing it through the forms of art, which is aesthetics.

Ethics has sometimes been called the knowledge of how to live, just as logic has been described as the knowledge of how to think. Another description of ethics is that it provides standards for the good life. There are several theories about what makes a life good. One of these is that pleasure, or happiness, is the thing to be sought. Happiness may be defined simply as prolonged pleasure, although no major thinker has ever considered dissipation as the highway to happiness. Various kinds of pleasure are recognized by different writers; pleasures of personal satisfaction are thought most important by some, social pleasures by others, and mental rather than physical pleasures by still others. A second theory of the good life is that virtue is the greatest good, with virtue defined as the full and proper use of one's abilities. According to this view, a person would get some of the greatest satisfactions from the education and development of his powers. A third view is that the good life rests on several bases rather than one.

Aesthetics deals with the principles of beauty and art. Various forms of beauty are considered such as productions in wood, stone, or sound, as well as the beauties of nature and of manners. There have been many theories of beauty. Socrates and Plato identified it with goodness and usefulness. Aristotle believed that the beautiful is that which excites immediate pleasure without arousing a desire for possession. A common definition is that beauty is the quality which gives unusual vividness to phenomenon and pleasure to the observer. Kant believed that the experience of beauty does not provide any knowledge, but that the appreciation it arouses in us is one aspect of our own mental activity. For Schopenhauer, who is one of the clearest writers on this topic, the experience of beauty involves an activity of contemplation that quiets the will to live for the moment so that we neither envy, desire, nor regret. Santayana stated that beauty is pleasure felt as the quality of a thing. For him, the frequent apprehension of beauty is one of the experiences necessary to make life worth living. Aesthetics is an important topic about which many books have been written.

Conclusion. The explanations of philosophy are so many and diverse that it is impossible even to catalogue all of them here. Many people, however, will want to read philosophy for themselves, feeling, as Socrates described it, that "an unexamined life is not worth living." For those not yet initiated into the subject it might be well to start with an interesting history of philosophy such as that of Will Durant. Another approach would be to begin with some division of philosophy, such as ethics. The student of philosophy will find his everyday thinking improved by both the ideas acquired and by the models of good reasoning with which he becomes familiar.

Explanation in Science. Just as we have found the primary method of philosophy to be that of reason we have found the scientific method to be that of observation. Although philosophers did not name science or recognize its separation from their discipline till the nineteenth century, primitive man experimented and observed. The medicinal value of many herbs was discovered before the time of written records and no one knows when, or by whom, quinine was first used. Indian corn, which today never grows wild, was domesticated so long ago that the original grass from which it developed is forgotten.

Science, today, is divided into the physical sciences based on physics and chemistry, along with the biological sciences which include the recently developing social sciences. The overlapping of sciences is so great that no universally accepted classification of them exists. If all the sciences were named, including those with rather specialized fields such as opthalmology, there would be a considerable number of them. We will limit ourselves here to pointing out a few of the main groups.

Physics. Physics has for its field the characteristics of all matter. The common divisions of the subject are those of mechanics, heat, light, sound, magnetism and electricity.

Chemistry. Chemistry has for its field the nature and composition of all kinds of matter and the changes it undergoes. The subject is usually divided into organic and inorganic chemistry. This division is an inheritance from alchemy when subjects were divided into groups according to their derivation as animal, vegetable, or mineral. Inorganic chemicals are of mineral origin and many, but not all, organic chemicals are of animal or vegetable origin. Organic chemistry deals exclusively with the compounds of carbon but as there are approximately a million of these compounds the organic chemist has his full share of labor. Inorganic chemistry is often grouped with astronomy and geology which illustrates the difficulty of classifying sciences as many problems that are not chemical are included in these disciplines.

Biology. Biology, which has for its field the characteristics of living matter, is divided into botony, the science of plant life, and zoology, the science of animal life. The distinction between these sciences is that plants can produce their own food while animals cannot. The social sciences of anthropology, psychology, sociology, economics and political science, dealing with the different aspects of the life of man, might be considered a branch or an appendage of biology. In the social sciences one finds a considerable use of statistics as a means of separating or establishing facts.

Summary.   There is no need to complete the list of sciences here, nor to name all the other subjects, such as history, where explanations of particular subject matter can be found. It has already been pointed out under the discussion of definition, that any subject which has been written about can be found in the indices. If a person wishes to think clearly about life's problems he must seek explanations that he cannot arrive at himself.

The philosophers will clarify for him many perplexities which can be analyzed and explained by the use of reason. The scientists, depending upon facts which they have gathered, defined, and classified, will explain his questions in terms of physical reality.

Chapter 6

COMMON ERRORS IN THINKING

An old saying declares that there is only one way to do a thing right, but that there are many ways to do it wrong. In the following pages are listed a number of ways to think incorrectly. A study of these will not necessarily enable a person to reach valid conclusions, but will sharpen his perception of error.

The errors enumerated here have been classified in eight groups.

1. Errors due to emotion and overpowering motivation.
2. Errors due to sense perception
3. Errors due to incomplete observation and memory
4. Errors due to suggestion
5. Errors due to ambiguity
6. Errors due to reasoning by analogy
7. Errors due to improper generalization
8. Errors in deductive procedure

ERRORS DUE TO EMOTION
AND OVERPOWERING MOTIVATION

Whenever a murder is done the detectives appear and ask, "What was the motive?" It is probable that the same method should be followed whenever some error in thinking is found. It is true that errors in thinking result from ignorance, carelessness and other causes, but the number of these is few compared with the errors due to such overpowering motivation as fear, avarice, jealousy, and ego-building.

Fear is never to be forgotten when the enemies of valid

thinking are enumerated. The coming of Space Men from Mars to kill or capture earthlings, the deterioration of human beings from eating food drawn from an impoverished earth, the destruction of the world through a war with atomic bombs have all been proclaimed.

Avarice is one of the sturdiest supporters of sly thinking. "How to make a million dollars in four easy lessons," is a kind of advice that is always available. The longing for beauty, strength, fine clothing and riches have led many a mind to mistaken conclusions. People want so many things. They want to know their own futures, whether proposed marriages will turn out well, whether children will be successful. They want to communicate with dear ones who have been taken by death. And why not, when the stars, the lines of the hand, the bumps on the head, the numbers attached to the letters of one's name, and the crystal balls interpreted by fortune tellers and "sensitive" mediums will provide the "facts" wanted. There are thousands of conscienceless fakers always ready to sell the public any soothing syrup it will buy.

Jealousy leads to mistaken evaluations of people. It is one of the main causes for the distorted facts spread in gossip. It is difficult for a jealous person to think honestly with all the facts.

Everywhere we find the "Great I Am." It is hard to become a real hero in the eyes of other people or to become a great leader of thought such as Einstein. Consequently, many people attempt this by false means. They claim to have found a "new cure for cancer" that the authorities are too bigoted to examine; or they discover that the earth is hollow inside with holes in it like the pores in the skin. Such people can explain how the world's problems should be solved and what is wrong with the universe. Some of them have devised ways to prolong life that work perfectly up to the moment of their untimely deaths.

But it is not enough to know that a good deal of bad thinking is motivated. A murder that has a motive is also cunningly perpetrated so that it will not be detected by the authorities. In the same way, bad thinking is apt to be processed by methods that camouflage it from the person who does the thinking and hide it from the public. It is these techniques that interest us here. Those given immediately below are the most obvious devices used although invalid thinking of other kinds may also be motivated.

Rationalization.   Rationalization is the mental process of elaborating or accepting false reasoning because it promises to satisfy some desire. A good example is found in the *Success Magazine* published by Orison Swett Marden from 1898 until he lost control of the publication in 1912. A few months before his publishing venture began, Marden was forty-eight years old, deep in debt, and the owner of a pawn ticket that had replaced his overcoat. As editor, however, Marden promised success to everyone who would apply his simple formula of will power, honesty, thrift and good nature. This rationalization of the assured attainment of everyone's dream brought a brief prosperity to its author. Marden's magazine thrived during the first years achieving a circulation of nearly 500,000. But the success formula was not adequate to assure the magazine's future, resulting in another failure for the editor. Marden tried to start a *New Success* magazine but death overtook him, still trying, in 1912.

A teen-age boy caught in a serious crime defended himself in this way. He said he had figured the danger and the penalty to be about the same for a minor crime and for a serious one. So he said, "You might as well choose the best." "Besides," he said, "there is satisfaction in doing a real man's job."

The correction for errors of rationalization is to determine whether the facts correspond with the generalization. Good-natured people are certainly found among the less successful as well as among the more successful. Nor does choosing the best, or taking satisfaction in a real man's job, lead logically to crime.

Logic-Tight Compartments.   Logic-tight compartments are aspects of life in which feeling is so intense that an individual is unable to think clearly about them. Values are so emotionally charged in these cases that a person can come to but one answer. Many people die without leaving wills because the thought of death is so horrible to them that they cannot face it. So they leave money that goes by default to the State or to relatives in whom they are not interested. To avoid speaking directly about death some people say that "John has passed away," and that "Sadie has sunk into an everlasting sleep." Rufus, who never stood up when he could sit, or sat when he could lie, has gone to his "well-deserved rest."

In dealing with logic-tight compartments we can correct our errors by viewing the facts objectively. This may be done by asking advice, by hiring a lawyer or other specialist, and sometimes just by a determined effort to examine the facts, no matter how much they hurt. In extreme cases the remedy lies in psychotherapy rather than in logic.

Prejudice. Prejudice is an area of thought in which the decisions have already been made on the basis of past conditioning, so that questions cannot be decided on the basis of their present merits. The concept of prejudice is familiar to everyone because of the attention that has been given recently to race prejudice. The feuds of Oriental and Occidental, of Jew and Gentile, and of Black and White go on and on. An example of prejudice brought to public attention is found in the argument between President Theodore Roosevelt and the Reverend Wm. J. Long the "nature faker". Reverend Long was a magazine writer who endowed animals with human characteristics, going so far as to declare that animals practiced a crude form of medicine among themselves. He wrote of one pet toad that enjoyed hymn music. President Roosevelt, who was prejudiced against any affectation or sentimentality in regard to animals, answered with a sharply critical article. Reverend Long, instead of replying to any of the president's arguments, attacked Roosevelt as a "Big Game Butcher." Then Roosevelt who had hunted big game in Africa but who could not stand, politically, the prejudice of the general public against the unnecessary killing of animals, withdrew. The explosive argument died down immediately without anybody's arguments being answered.

Emotionally-Toned Words. Words carry both information and feeling, and sometimes the latter pushes the former out. Emotional words are provocative. They are not conductive to the calmness that is necessary for sound reasoning, consequently they have led to many an invalid conclusion. "I don't see how anybody in his right mind can follow your thinking," says one person in an argument. "There is something overwrought, peculiar, and unbalanced in what you say. As I understand it, you want us to renounce all we have done and go back to our position of last year."

In order to prevent unwise decisions from being made as a result of emotionally-toned words, we should delete such words from a proposition and then examine what is left. In the case above the remainder would be, "You want us to go back to our position of last year." This phrase suggests that there might be reasons for the action, and a factual search for these reasons would probably provide the basis for some sound thinking.

Begging the Question. Begging a question is assuming a conclusion without proving it while covering up the error with emotional confusion. This is probably done by everyone who gets into an argument, but it is a common trick of lawyers attempting to influence a jury. "Gentlemen," they will say, "you represent a town that it has taken years of hard work to build. It is the haven of your wives and children. The defendant has committed murder here among your homes. Any verdict other than guilty will endanger your whole community."

It is, of course, the lawyer's duty to prove that the man is a murderer. But if he calls him one he may influence the jury to believe he is one even though he has not proved it.

Probably the most extravagant example of begging the question today is provided by the Communists. Almost daily they claim that they are "riding the wave of the future" and that capitalistic societies are dying. This, however, is the whole question being decided. Private enterprise has by no means been proved more inept than dictatorship. Only time can tell which system will "ride the wave of the future."

The cure for this kind of error is to strike the question-begging words from the record. One must ask what facts have been given and precisely how they are related to the generalization or conclusion named.

Including Evidence not Pertinent to the Question. If a person includes irrelevant evidence favorable to his purpose he may bias a conclusion. A common instance of this occurs when a lawyer brings up a man's past as evidence, instead of sticking to the facts of a particular instance. A man who has been in jail three times is more likely to be sent there again than is a man who has never been in jail. In applying for a responsible job a man who must put on his application blank the fact that he has been arrested and fined is less likely to get the job than one who need not make such an admission. A person who has received a ticket for speeding and who carries a statement of this on his driver's license is more likely to be given another ticket than is a person with a clean record.

Criminals sometimes reform and become good. Also, many people who would lie would not steal, and many who would steal will not murder. Justice requires that a defendant be judged in each case separately. When a criminal record is held against a person who is being tried for a crime, this error is invited.

To prevent this error from occuring, bring out sharply the individual nature of the present situation. Each crime should be examined exclusively on its own evidence.

Conclusions Influenced by Consequences to the Individual. Many Russians, Hungarians, Poles, and Cubans in the United States who left their families in their native countries have had to be very careful not to reveal any damaging facts about their home governments. Thus, facts remain hidden because their revelation could lead to unpleasant consequences. Similarly, prisoners in communistic countries who wanted to keep from freezing to death, who wanted to eat, or who wanted to open a channel to freedom, had to think, or, at least, speak, in certain prescribed ways.

This error of drawing conclusions on the basis of the consequences to the individual rather than on facts is, however, not always a matter of life and death. It influences disputes between labor and management. Also in politics, the labor bloc tends to weigh certain facts more heavily, whereas the farm bloc considers other factors more important. Honest people often find themselves on the opposite sides of a question in situations like this because their practical interests have influenced their thinking.

Mob Rule. Thinking by mob rule consists in losing one's independence to the dictates of a mob. Everyone has a limit to the time he can stand alone against his environment, and in some cases this limit is low.

Recently, in New York a seventeen-year-old boy, planning to be a paratrooper, was walking with his gang across a bridge. The gang started to tease the boy about his qualifications for parachute jumping. He was "yellow." He didn't have the nerve. He would "chicken out." Flushed with anger, the boy vaulted the four-foot railing of the bridge and pulled off his shirt. "I'll show you," he cried, and jumped. It was 180 feet to the river below and this foolhardiness proved fatal.

Every country has a day to parade its military strength. When a man watches an apparently endless column of soldiers marching before him, with airplanes overhead and tanks rolling by, he can hardly imagine any force great enough to challenge them. When thousands of people in close formation shout, "Heil Hitler!" it requires a good deal of determination to resist.

The cure for mob rule is personal self-reliance.

Attacking the person instead of the argument. This error needs little definition. It consists of turning the attention away from the facts in an argument to the people participating in it. Reformers and people defending unpopular causes usually experience this fate. It is often easier to attack an individual than an argument. Thus, in many political campaigns candidates have refused to discuss issues and have preferred to engage in "mud slinging." President Hoover was blamed for the depression that came in his administration by people who found it much easier to blame Hoover than to understand the problems involved. It is also a common dodge in debates to avoid argument by criticizing the people supporting it. Issues, however, should be discussed on the basis of their own merits.

ERRORS OF SENSE PERCEPTION

Since our minds work as a unit, it is difficult for an individual to separate the factors in a situation. When the senses bring evidence contradictory to reason, the sensory elements which seem immediate and clear are often accepted as correct.

Consequently, used automobiles put up for sale are often polished until they shine. Many people cannot tell the difference between a shiny car and a good one. Vegetable oil substitutes for butter are usually colored like butter when the law permits, so that the public will feel they contain that "rich, cream-packed nutrition." Oranges are often colored to look as people suppose oranges ought to look. People dress up when they go job hunting since personnel men cannot see a clean heart but are often impressed by a clean shirt. It has been found that the average bishop is taller than the average minister, the average college president is taller than the average professor, and the average executive is taller than his average worker, although intelligence tests and other measurements show little correspondence between height and ability.

The diagrams below illustrate how sensory illusions can be used to support arguments. It is done here merely by rotating the position of the diagram.

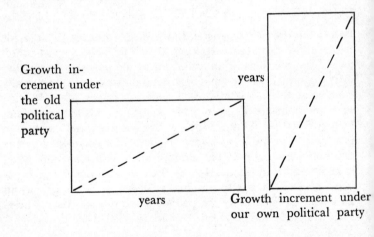

The rate of growth illustrated is exactly the same in the two diagrams

In a second example below, income earned by the old **and** new managements are compared. Incidentally the income was exactly the same.

Income under the backward-looking old management (The straight line measures the income) 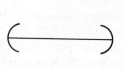 Income under the forward-looking new management (The straight line measures the income)

Examples of illusions used to deceive the enemy in war are endless. In the Civil War, General Beauregard trimmed tree trunks to look like cannon, leading the Yankees under McClellan to think his army greater than it was. The illusions of camouflage were used widely in World Wars I and II to conceal ships at sea as well as to hide ammunition dumps and army camps ashore. Today many military installations are camouflaged to prevent them from being identified from the air.

Errors of sense perception operate in an insidious way since the individual is usually not aware that his sensations are misleading him. The cure for this error is to stop, look, listen and measure. Sometimes an error passed over by one person will be picked up by another. Fortunately an error of this kind, once found, is acknowledged. It is seldom the subject of a debate.

ERRORS DUE TO INCOMPLETE OBSERVATION AND MEMORY

Failure to get the facts because they are either observed carelessly or taken unchecked from a defective memory are among the most frequent causes of poor thinking. For instance, Rousseau and Voltaire were contemporary French philosophers who disagreed on their ideas of primitive life. Rousseau believed that primitive life was simple, sane, healthy and desirable. The evils of life, he believed, were contributed by the complexities and corruptions of civilization. His theory of civilization was organized around this view. The best book that had ever been written, said Rousseau, was not a treatise of Aristotle, but "Robinson Crusoe". Voltaire, on the other hand, believed that primitive life was savage, dirty and short. He threw the weight of his influence on the side of all the complexities of civilized refinement. Neither philosopher ever made a factual study of primitive life to determine the truth of the facts on which his thinking was based.

Many people make the same mistake in regard to childhood. It is common to think of the days of youth as "boyhood's time of June." In his poem "The Barefoot Boy," Whittier grows ecstatic and credits these years with "outward sunshine, inward joy!" But social workers and psychologists who deal directly with children, listening to their problems, say that childhood, particularly the years of adolescence represented by the barefoot boy, is anything but a time of inward joy. All the rules of a determined society bear down on the child. Some children respond easily, but others do not. Any philosophy based on the idea that childhood is always a time of happiness is certain to be mistaken.

The cure for errors due to poor observation and unchecked memory is obvious but difficult. Do the spade work and get the facts.

ERRORS DUE TO SUGGESTION

Suggestion. Suggestion is characterized by the presentation of an idea rather than by making a reasoned argument. Responding without thought may lead to sensible action as well as error, depending upon circumstances. By the side of a national highway in New Jersey someone erected a tombstone inscribed "Drive Carefully," suggesting that a careless person might end up under a tombstone. This suggestion was well taken, but suggestion can, and often does, lead to serious error. Some years ago the idea of a flying saucer alarmed many people, convincing them that they were being watched by Communists or perhaps by strange beings from outer space. The United States Air Force carried on an expensive eight-year investigation to quiet these fears. A citizen's respect for police officers has been taken advantage of many times. In Brooklyn a thug dressed in a stolen police uniform demanded, and received, one thousand dollars from a house painter. Even more important are the cases of primitive people subordinating themselves to their witch doctors. In Uganda two little girls, six and three years old, were killed for their hand and heel bones used in magic rites. The perpetrators were known by the tribesmen but, influenced by the impressive ceremonies of the medicine men suggesting superhuman powers, these primitive people refused to give the evidence necessary to convict the witch doctors.

Repeated Affirmation and Prestige. The common techniques in the use of suggestion are repetition and the use of prestige, as in using titles merely to impress people. Repetition is used particularly in propaganda where one often meets with the belief that if a lie is repeated often enough it will be believed. This seems to be true whenever opposing evidence can be concealed. Prestige also is suggestive. Children are accustomed to believing their parents, which leads them, as they grow up, to transfer this faith to anyone of power or position.

Overconfidence. Overconfidence leads a person to accept enticing suggestions without investigating them. Young people accustomed to success in a local environment as well as over-enthusiastic theorists are probably the most subject to this weakness. The *Titanic* was the largest passenger ship of its day. It was the first great passenger ship with airtight compartments guaranteed to keep it afloat. No matter what happened, it was thought, so few of these compartments could be damaged at one time that the remaining ones would float the ship. It was considered unsinkable. Consequently, the captain drove the *Titanic* through the fog at such a speed that when it did hit an iceberg it sank in a few hours.

When Amelia Earhart flew over the Pacific, she had a good plane and a trustworthy companion, but she failed to consider the dangers of landing in alien lands. It is believed now, at least by some, that she landed on an island where every intruder was shot as a spy.

Lack of Confidence and Fear. Lack of confidence and fear lead one to accept eagerly any suggestions that promise security. For this reason, many people vote themselves aid from the Federal Government, forgetting that they will have to pay for it later, and many other people have voted away their entire freedom, yielding to some dictator who made vague promises of protecting them from want.

ERRORS DUE TO AMBIGUITY

The errors of ambiguity are almost always errors in the careless use of language. There are a number of ways by which a person can entangle himself in his own words.

Confusing Whole and Part. Parts do not always represent the wholes from which they come, nor a whole its parts. Sometimes young people choose careers because of one aspect of the occupation that attracts them; doctors have prestige, bankers work in fine buildings, forest rangers can enjoy being out in the woods the whole day long, and sailors see the world. Such parts do not truly represent the whole occupation.

In contrast to this, people sometimes take the description of the whole and apply it to the part. The United States, it is said, has a higher standard of living than any other nation. So here is Mr. Jones, a citizen of the United States, whom we consequently assume has a higher standard of living than any citizen of any other nation. Again, it is said that California has a wonderful climate where elderly people may retire in comfort. In consequence, many people go there to live, in some cases without carefully selecting the spot to which they go. They forget that California also has mountains and deserts, including Death Valley, one of the hottest and driest climates in the world, as well as Feather River Canyon and Donner Pass, where people have frozen to death.

Technical Jargon. Technical jargon does not refer to the use of technical words among professionals who employ such terms to save time and give specific meaning to what they say, but to the use of technical terms to impress or confuse the general public. Sometimes professional people use such jargon to influence their clients. Patent medicines are often described in such high-sounding but meaningless phrases. A certain patent medicine has three elements to its name, the first two being "Neo-Aqua." This means "new" or "recent" water, but many of the people who buy the product do not know this. Another advertisement claims that its product is "clinically" tested by doctors, although few people would understand just what this means. Another claim is that a pill is an "exclusive anti-allergent to block allergic reactions." Such use of words that suggest technical knowledge impresses many people.

The correction of this error is to debunk the jargon. But when changing jargon into simple English, be sure to get a correct translation.

Confusing Categories that Merge. How many colored ancestors does it take to make a man a Negro, and how many Caucasian ancestors to make a man a Caucasian? Men have tried to draw lines between races and also between classes. They have tried to put other men into categories of being either rich or poor, educated or uneducated, high-brow or low-brow. Yet there are no clear-cut lines between social classes, races, or between neighborhoods.

A problem that frequently reaches the newspaper headlines is whether a teacher may use "physical restraint" with a pupil. At what point does an application of the birch rod cease being disciplinary and become cruelty? There is no precise dividing line between beneficial punishment and revengeful punishment. A similar question is the age at which a person should be allowed to vote. In Georgia the voting age is eighteen, in most of the United States it is twenty-one. Is there a particular age before which people are not responsible and after which they are?

It is human nature to make distinctions, such as those above, in continuous data. But many errors are sure to follow. The correction of these errors, insofar as they can be corrected, lies in measurement and statistics. But in such problems as a man's race or his virtue it is not easy to apply the remedies named. In many cases of this kind the answers are not logical but emotional. The best solution sometimes may be to seek objectivity in advice or professional counseling.

Words Used in Different Senses. One word is often made to serve many purposes. Usually the context, the gestures, or the inflection completes the meaning and makes clear what is indicated. But sometimes the meaning is not clear, and often it is made ambiguous with a definite purpose. In this way thinking is often carelessly or intentionally led astray. The examples below are not very serious, but they indicate what can be done.

A new motion picture company was named "The Miracle Film Company." Then a slogan for the company was sought, and this one was proposed: "If it's a good picture it's a Miracle."

A familiar old ditty goes something like this:
The fisherman plays for the fun of the game
And his catch may be heavy or light,
But the stories he tells would bring anyone fame,
As he lies by the fire at night.

A remedy for errors resulting from using words with a double meaning is to require a restatement and suspend one's thinking until the facts have been made clear.

Oral Omissions. Business interview and conversational data is replete with information that is inadequate because part of the subject matter is omitted. "Frank lacks skill." What kind of skill? "John has not had enough experience." Experience for what? "Sally won't do, she's not serious enough." Not serious enough for what? When the speaker is gone so that he cannot be questioned further, such partial information can lead to serious errors if the suggestions given are followed. Executives and others who prefer getting their facts from interview material and oral briefing rather than from reading must make sure that the information given them is complete.

Breaking up the Logic. It is difficult to persist in a consecutive train of thought. Lawyers and debaters sometimes make this still more difficult for their opponents by breaking up the train of thought. Almost any interruption will do this. Two common interruptions that are within the rules are to pretend not to understand some simple point or to ask for repeated explanations until the main problem is lost among the distractions. A similar technique is to pick out some term and call for a definition, not because a meaning is unknown, but because an interruption in the train of thought is wanted.

ERRORS DUE TO REASONING BY ANALOGY

More solutions to human problems and also more errors have come from thinking by analogy than from any other technique. Analogies are highly prized as a means of developing hypotheses, even though they are not helpful in verification. One needs only to consider our treatment of pets to see how much we think by comparison. Animals cannot speak or tell us directly what they are feeling, but we conclude from their actions that they are feeling as we would feel if we acted in a similar way. The result seems to be satisfactory.

Usually the similarity rests on one factor, and there are many elements that differ. Therefore, a conclusion based on the one similar factor may be misleading. Primitive people do many curious and useless things based on reasoning by analogy. When planting grain they often have the seed sown by a woman who has had many children, believing this will guaranty fertility. When they wish to injure a person they often make an image of him and destroy it. When a person dies they bury his tools with him, anticipating that his future life will be like the life he has lived. A skeleton was found, in one of the old Etruscan tombs, still clutching a coin put in his hand to pay his fare across the river Styx.

More modern examples of thinking by analogy would include the descriptions by Jules Verne in his book *20,000 Leagues Under the Sea*. Jules Verne forsaw many devices but none of his ideas were useful in a practical way since they were only analogous to things already known. The world had to wait for the development of inventions based on cause and effect. Mark Twain lost a fortune when he backed a project to print newspapers with a machine that was the analogue of the typewriter. When Hans Christian Andersen, author of *Mother Goose Stories for Children,* was in England, Charles Dickens found him in tears over some personal critism he had read in the papers. Dickens made a deep mark in the sand with his foot saying, "This is criticism." Then he erased it adding "Thus it disappears."

Analogies are usually composed of both truth and error. In some ways criticism is like a mark in the sand, in other ways it is not. It is as in the common phrase, "She eats like a bird." From one point of view she is said to eat little; from another, if she eats like a bird she eats her weight in food every day. If one sees the truth in an analogy he is enlightened. If his mind is misled by the error he will be mistaken.

The correction of errors due to reasoning by analogy is never to verify thinking by this means. Analogies are very useful in creative thinking, but in verification they often lead one astray. It is said that nothing can be proved by analogy. Verify the conclusion by direct observation of cause and effect.

Guilt by Association.   It is an old opinion that "Birds of a feather flock together." There is a common tendency to assume that a person is like his associates. Such assumptions are, however, often false. Because a person has been seen with a Communist, it does not necessarily follow that he is a Communist himself. A person who marries into a family one of whose members belongs to the Ku Klux Klan does not necessarily approve of the Klan. The human race is perverse in that it tends to believe that anyone who lives with thieves is also a thief, though it does not believe everyone who lives with philosophers is a philosopher. The correction for error due to guilt by association is found in investigating each individual. Since people are often ruined by irresponsible charges, claims of guilt should be verified and proved before they are published.

ERRORS DUE TO IMPROPER GENERALIZATION

Generalizations describe groups of facts and are usually made before all the facts have been counted. In assuming that the groups will be completed with instances like those already observed, a person may be cautious and assume too little, thus failing to include suitable instances, or be rash and assume too much. The pattern that Mr. Butterick made for his wife represents a case where proper generalization was too limited. Mr. Butterick, a tailor, arranged a paper pattern to help his wife make dresses for their daughter. It was very effective and they were satisfied. But it was not until a neighbor, Mrs. Jones Warren Wilder, borrowed the pattern and her husband saw its possibilities that the idea developed of making paper patterns for the market. Out of Wilder's generalization regarding the value of Mr. Butterick's pattern the famous Butterick

Pattern Co. was founded in 1880. In limiting the pattern to his daughter's dresses Mr. Butterick failed to make a proper generalization. But it is in assuming too much, or over-generalization that most errors occur.

Extension of the Generalization. If the generalization is extended beyond the facts that it describes, it becomes false and its use leads to error.

A common example of over-generalization is found when a person assumes that his own individual formula for health or success will apply equally to all other persons. Thus, an octogenarian may attribute his old age to smoking a cigar a day, or a successful business man may attribute his success to rising at five o'clock every morning. It is, however, far from true that a cigar a day is healthful for everyone, nor will rising at five o'clock make everyone a successful business man. Unguarded generalizations from a limited past experience to future experience, or from what is true in one environment to what will be true in other environments are very common. Every generalization is a description of a particular group of facts. When the generalization is made to apply beyond those facts it is subject to error.

Tabloid Thinking. Since most situations in life are compounded of various facts, a great many rules have exceptions. Disregarding all exceptions and describing everything in bold terms has sometimes been called "Tabloid Thinking." Newspapers that are written in this vein make broad claims of problem-solving that conceal all the difficulties. One newspaper, for example, promises its readers that "spare parts banks" for human hearts and lungs are to be set up soon in two of the largest cities of the United States. The article mentions some of the difficulties that have been encountered in doing this but says such difficulties are nearly solved. Another article promises a "memory machine" that will detect a man's every thought and record all he knows. In a short time, it says, all the ideas of every genius and near-genius will be automatically recorded, digested, and applied to the solution of the world's problems. This machine is nearly perfected, says the article, and will appear on the market almost any day.

Tabloid thinking is all in big strokes. It promises great

things, or threatens in expansive terms, and misleads by concealing all the difficulties in the way of its conclusions. (Everybody will be killed by atomic bombs). The remedy for this kind of thinking is to look behind the scenes. Examine the difficulties and look for the facts and arguments that might be used by the opposition.

ERRORS IN DEDUCTIVE PROCEDURES

Deduction is all a matter of relationships, having nothing to do with determining the truth of the facts, or the reliability of the generalizations. Errors that are due to the statement of invalid relationships are errors in deduction.

Diversion to Another Topic. One of the simplest ways to get away from a difficulty or unpleasant line of reasoning is to move to another topic.

A teacher asked a child, "If you can buy a barrel of cider for one dollar, how many can you buy for five dollars?"

"I wouldn't buy that many," answered the child. "It's sour."

In complex problems it is usually easy to divert the attention from the main problem to a subordinate problem. A discussion of the adequate defense of the United States can easily deteriorate into an argument as to whether the Army or the Air Force should have charge of the missile program. A discussion of sales in business can turn into a debate as to whether a slow period is a "seasonal decline," a "recession," or a setback due to last year's strike. Sometimes subordinate questions must be discussed, but if they are allowed to divert all the thinking away from the main topic, the error of diversion results.

The "Middle-of-the-Road" Error. Somebody can be found taking an extreme position on almost every issue. There is no logical reason why one of these extremes might not be the right position. But the accusation that a man is either too radical or too reactionary assumes that the middle position is probably nearer the truth.

Basing an argument not on fact, but merely on moderation, brings about this error. When a person has an advanced case of cancer, the only possible cure may be a major operation. A minor operation, though more moderate, would be useless. The mere fact that something is moderate is as irrelevant as the fact that something else is radical. In each case, our conclusion must be based on facts.

Argument in a Circle.   A circular argument is the confusion of cause and effect with synonyms. Thus, we would not be reasoning but playing with words if we argued that a man is thrifty because he saves his money and saves his money because he is thrifty. Thrift is the description of a group of actions. If one wants to understand thrift, one must examine these actions and the circumstances that give rise to them. To correct a circular argument, one must get out of the circle and go back to the facts.

Speculative Thinking.   Speculative thinking begins with a theory for which truth is claimed. Then, all facts and arguments are forced into line with the theory. The most famous case of speculative thinking today is the "party line" of the Communists. It is assumed that the theories of Marx, Engels, and Lenin are true and consequently all communistic thinking must conform to these theories. The "party line" has caused a great deal of trouble for original thinkers of all kinds in communistic countries since facts must be manipulated to conform to political doctrine.

The Exception Proves the Rule.   Almost all rules and generalizations have exceptions, but if too many exceptions are found, there is soon no rule. Therefore, the exception *tests* the rule. The word *"proves,"* from the Latin *probare* meant, as it still does in some contexts, that the exception tries out the rule and "puts it on probation." No exception proves a rule in terms of verification, although the phrase has come to be so used as a sort of flippant formula.

The error involved here is corrected by pointing out that exceptions do not verify rules and that a formula is no substitute for a fact.

Proof by Inconsequent Argument.   Arguments may seem reasonable when in fact no direct consequences have been determined. One of the most famous inconsequent arguments ever made was that of Bishop Wilberforce, who, when arguing against Darwinian Evolution, asked Thomas Huxley on which side of his family he claimed descent from a monkey. Another instance, and one which caused much more trouble occurred when Dr. Harvey Wiley, father of the Federal Pure Food and Drugs Act was fighting to keep alum out of baking powder, narcotics out of babies' medicine, coal tar dyes out of butter and jam, and other poisons out of food. The main argument used against Dr. Wiley was that he was attempting to take away from people one of their main constitutional rights, their freedom to eat whatever they choose.

Joseph S. Newman has pointed out a case of inconsequent argument by modifying a nursery rhyme.

> Peter Peter Pumpkin eater
> Had a wife and couldn't keep her.
> Peter sadly shook his head
> "Damn inflation!" Peter said.

Sometimes critics are wrong in believing that cause and effect is other than it is. A small boy was being described. "Is he dumb!" said one. "If you let him choose between a fifty-cent piece and a quarter, he'll always choose the quarter. I've seen it tried a dozen times."

A business man standing nearby heard this remark, tested out the boy, and found the statement true. So he set about to educate the youngster. "Don't you know," he said, "that a fifty-cent piece is more than a quarter? Any sensible person would choose the fifty-cent piece."

"Yeah," said the boy, "but if I did that people would stop playing the game with me."

To avoid this error of failing to recognize the authentic cause and effect relationships, examine Mills Methods. (Page 33)

Misleading with a Name. Many people have thought that nothing was more certain than death and taxes, but even taxes have now been removed. "The Soviet Union is a country without taxes," claims an article in the July, 1960 monthly magazine *USSR*. "The riddance by 1965 of all direct taxes on the Soviet population is the final step in the systematic policy of tax abolition." Of course the Soviet Union will need as much revenue as ever, but this will come from the "profits of state enterprise." Everyone knows that profits are legitimate and pleasant, and so it does not matter that the Soviet Union is a great monopoly and charges such profits as it sees fit. The increased prices, however, are nothing but a form of taxation, no matter what the name.

To correct this error remember that "A rose by any other name would smell as sweet."

Some Invalid Syllogisms. Invalid means unproven. Sometimes the conclusion of an invalid syllogism can be sound, as when two errors correct each other. Whenever there are errors, however, it is safer to find, and correct them, than to take a chance with the result. Perhaps the reader would like to find the errors in the following syllogisms.

He who has nothing, fears nothing
Joe fears nothing
Therefore Joe has nothing.

Nearly all rocks are heavy
Many rocks contain granite
Therefore some things containing granite are heavy.

All hummingbirds fly fast
All hummingbirds have wings
Therefore all objects that fly fast have wings.

A noun is not a pronoun
A noun is not an adjective
Therefore no pronouns are adjectives.

No evil can happen to a good man
Joe is not a good man
Therefore evil will happen to him.

Poverty is the parent of revolution and crime
Ignorance is the parent of revolution and crime
Therefore ignorance is poverty

INDEX OF NAMES

SUBJECT INDEX

Administration, 114.
Aesthetics, 120
Alexandria, 21
Algebra, Boole's, 59
Ambiguous design, 39
Ambivert, 26
American Medical
    Association, 21
Analogy, 46
Annuity, 47
Arabs, 21
Argument in a circle, 141
Aristotelian thinking, 66, 67
Artist, 23
Associational possibilities, 101
Astrology, 2
Astronomer, 40
Atmosphere effect, 71
Authority, 22, 60
Autosuggestion, 3

Bias, 60
Biology, 121, 122
Board of experts, 27
Books, 24
Borderline, 27
Botany, 121
Brain machines, 59
Breaking up logic, 136
Bureau of standards, 6
Business conference, 111

Cancer, 30, 39, 40
Categories, Aristotle, 90
Categories, emotional, 91
Categories, functional, 91
Categories, Hegel, 91
Categories, Immanuel Kant, 91
Chemistry, 24, 29, 38, 121
Cigarettes, 39, 40
Class, 17, 23
    ideas of, 11
    merging classes, 135

Classification, 1, 25, 41
    Dewey Decimal System, 106
    index, 25
    Library of Congress System,
        106
    miscellaneous items, 28
    natural, rules, 25
    overlapping, 28
    principles, 25
    subdivided, 25
    two principles at once,
        25, 26, 28
Clairvoyance, 21
Clinical method, 37, 39
Communication, 67
Communists, 67
Computers, 59
Concepts, 1, 15, 16, 18, 19, 23,
    64, 68
    high level, 13, 14, 15, 101
    low level, 13, 14, 15
    morality, 15
    nature of, 10, 11, 12, 13
Conclusion, 80, 81
Consistency, 21
Contradiction, law of, 64, 65
Control group, 38
Conversion, 76
Correlation, 59
Counseling, 111
Creative act, 30
Creativity, formula, 99
Culture, 102
Cum laude, 27, 28

Data, continuous, 66
Data, discrete, 66
Decision making, 111
Deduction, 1, 18, 88
    definition of, 62, 105
    errors, 140
    logic, 63
Defense of the country, 24